You Can Heal After Tragic Loss

A 45 Day Guidebook to Controlled Grief

Dr. Cristi Bundukamara, Ed. D PMHNP

Knowing When to Seek Professional Help

There are times in our lives when professional help is needed. We encourage you to seek professional help when you desire to do so or when you are having significant symptoms.

This includes diagnoses like schizophrenia, bipolar, depression and anxiety, or evidence of mania, and others.

If you are struggling with:

Suicidal thoughts *(thoughts of harming yourself)*, **Homicidal thoughts** *(thoughts of harming someone else)*, **Audio or Visual hallucinations** *(hearing or seeing things that no one else can see or hear)* or **other symptoms of mental health impairment,**

Please seek professional help IMMEDIATELY

National Suicide Prevention Lifeline
(24 Hour Hotline) 1-800-273-8255

Crisis Text Line
Text HOME to 741741 - for free, 24/7 crisis support in the US

Visit Your Local Emergency Room

Our Mission

To inspire all humanity to embrace the journey of mental strength.

www.mentallystrong.com

Table of Contents

Introduction

Congratulations on taking the first step along your Controlled Grief journey. I, Cristi Bundukamara (Dr. B.), will be your guide. I understand what you're going through because I am a mental health professional, but even more importantly, I have also suffered unimaginable loss. Many believe that there is a set time to grieve or that you should get over it and move on after six months or so. The truth is that it's actually healthy to grieve. And you can do it in a controlled way, one that doesn't wreak havoc on your life, and allows you to function and engage in everyday activities.

This book was written with that goal in mind: to enable you to go on your own Controlled Grief journey. Whether you've lost a child or children (like me), a spouse, a friend, a relative, or something else that was important to you, you can apply the activities in this workbook to your own grief process.

As a guide for your journey, I've included experiences from my 45-day Controlled Grief pilgrimage along with suggested activities for you to complete each day. The 45-day timeline is not to imply that you should only grieve for 45 days and then be done with it. On the contrary, it's merely a period of time that I chose to personally dedicate to actively grieve (and use as a framework for this book). You don't have to complete your 45 days consecutively either, however, I found that consecutive days allowed for deeper healing. Grief is a very personal thing, so choose the schedule and timeline that works best for you.

While working through these activities, you are not only going to learn about my Controlled Grief journey but also what I discovered about *how to grieve*. As part of my process, I'd hoped to come up with *a way to grieve properly* and find my truth (that was the main theme). I did, and during my journey, I also uncovered 5 Self's related to grieving. They are Self-Care, finding your Spiritual Self, Self-Improvement through study, Self-Regulation, and Self-Movement. These concepts came to me prior to starting the 45 days of grief, but I further developed them as I moved along.

Primarily, I tried to hone in on my Spiritual Self, including my relationship with God and other existential beliefs. If your experience has been like mine, you may be spiritually stuck or have been left questioning your faith. There are things that you can do to move forward in this regard, although the idea of moving forward can be a trigger for anyone, especially those that have lost a child or someone else very dear to them. If I'm being honest with you, I still don't completely want to move forward. I want my children back instead, but I know that is not possible, so I've been forced to dig deeper.

During the 45 days, it came to me that I really struggled because I do have a belief in God, but at the same time, I'm also very angry at God. So, there was this spiritual battle that boiled down to finding my truth. I want to challenge you as you begin your own journey to think about and write down what you know to be true. Then similarly capture what you used to believe was true or what you no longer believe to be true. With the intense pain that you are experiencing, it will be crucial to find the truth for yourself.

I have grown significantly in these 45 days of grief, and will continue to grow, but the pain is still there, and that's okay. What's not okay is to wallow or ruminate in it. That's why we must focus on another self, Self-Regulation. It involves our ability to take time for Controlled Grief and to be able to get back to our day once we are done.

During your journey, it will also be very helpful to engage in Self-Improvement through study. As part of my own Self-Improvement, I reviewed several books on grief as well as a number of grief theories. Although grief doesn't involve a natural, linear process (like many of the theories suggest), there are nuggets of information that you can learn and grow from while you study. As you move through your days, continue to try to find information that's going to help you improve, no matter what type of information that is.

Self-Movement is another of the 5 Self's that I identified. You must process trauma and pain related to grief, but what does that really mean? Self-Movement is the conscious physical movement of the body to energetically push out pain. Will that pain ever be completely gone? No, but so many grieving friends, parents, and spouses have not been able to move forward because they are not releasing that pain from their bodies at all.

Finally, the last self is Self-Care which involves taking care of yourself as you go through this intense process. It's vital that you address your personal well-being as you might have been ignoring it for some time or have neglected it due to the intense sorrow that you've experienced. Self-care can come in numerous forms including sleeping in, taking naps, going to a spa, hanging out with friends, and more (whatever makes you feel whole). Ensure that you are placing an emphasis on meeting your own self-care needs as you embark on your Controlled Grief journey.

During each of the 45 days, I focused on engaging in Controlled Grief activities related to these 5 Self's (Spiritual Self, Self-Improvement, Self-Movement, Self-Care, and Self-Regulation). I began with a morning meditation (Spiritual Self). Throughout the book, I speak of having a relationship with God and about being very angry with Him. You will also notice that I use many different spiritual modalities. I am not sharing my experience as absolute truth but am instead sharing it as my truth. During your journey, I want to encourage you to find your own spiritual self, path, and truth.

I then moved on to focus on a grief theory or to gather information from a grief-related book or resource (Self-Improvement). After that, I participated in a Controlled Grief activity such as going through pictures of my children. Next, I took part in some type of Self-Movement which involved physical motion to help move the grief forward (yoga, gymnastics, walking on the treadmill, etc.). Then, I participated in a Self-Care activity (had a massage, indulged in a treat, went out, etc.). Finally, as a last step, I worked on my Self-Regulation and coming back to center to get on with my day.

While using this workbook, you will participate in the following similar daily activities:

- o Read About My Experience
- o Engage in a Controlled Grief Activity
- o Complete a Morning Meditation or Prayer (Spiritual Self)
- o Become Familiar with a Grief Theory/Information (Self-Improvement)
- o Participate in a Physical Activity (Self-Movement)
- o Practice Self-Care (Self-Care)
- o Engage in a Self-Regulation Activity to Get Back to Your Day (Self-Regulation)
- o Journal Your Own Experience and/or Complete Choice Opportunities

It is my sincere wish, that at the end of your 45-day period, you will have begun to incorporate controlled grieving into your life and have the tools necessary to grieve and process the loss that you've experienced, becoming mentally stronger in the process.

The Mentally Strong Method

Throughout this workbook, I will be referring to and including information and worksheets related to the Mentally STRONG Method which can be applied to grief. I created the Mentally STRONG Method because I truly believe we can strengthen our brains. Mental strength is an attribute we admire in people; however, we do not teach it in any standard curriculum. This method is scientifically backed by cognitive behavioral theories and empowers you to gain insight, resilience, and mental strength on your lifetime journey of self-improvement. The Mentally STRONG Method is a simple and practical method which utilizes evidence-based research as its foundation in the form of cognitive- behavioral therapy. You can find out more about the Mentally Strong Method in the Appendix at the back of this workbook and/or by taking one of our Mentally STRONG Method courses. We also train Mentally STRONG Ambassadors and coaches as well.

What are Choice Opportunities?

Choice Opportunities are worksheets that we use in the Power of Choice element of the Mentally STRONG Method. They are exactly what the title infers; an opportunity to make a choice to heal in a specific category. The Choice Opportunities I've provided in this book are specific to the grief category. I created many of them along my own personal grief journey.

Dr. B's Story

In order to understand my mission and method, I feel that it's important for you to first become familiar with my personal story and firsthand experience with grief. I met my husband and got married in 1997. Over time, my family grew, and my heart did too. Our diverse household included myself, my husband (Bundy), two biological mixed-race children (Reggie and Miah), and five adopted children (Nidra, Johnny, Cristina, Kayla, and Cory). With each new addition, I felt lucky and blessed. I believed that God had a special plan for me. But when a senseless tragedy followed by a devastatingly rare and difficult-to-diagnose genetic disorder struck my family, it challenged my view of life, my mental strength, and my faith in God.

You see, grief has not been a stranger to me. In fact, it's had a consistent presence in my life. I've faced unimaginable losses that began when one of my adopted sons, Johnny, passed away in a drowning accident. After that, both of my biological children (one after the other) lost their lives to DRPLA (the rare genetic disorder that I mentioned earlier). My husband, Bundy, is still currently struggling with DRPLA, and I am experiencing anticipatory grief as a result.

It goes without saying, of course, that life is filled with joy and pain, in varying degrees, for different people. But, if I'm being honest, I feel that I've had more than my fair share of both. Do I feel singled out? Sometimes. Have I ever wallowed in my grief and felt sorry for myself? Yes. Have I ever gotten permanently stuck there? No. With each new blow, I've found a way to move forward, process my grief, and to make the choice to keep going. Through my experience and those of the many patients who I've worked with over the years, I recognize that people are immensely resilient. We all have the choice to find mental strength, to love, to hope, to persevere, and to never give up. I appreciate that while I have experienced heart-wrenching setbacks, I have relied on my family for comfort and support, and we have all grown mentally stronger as a result.

This workbook is my personal journey through the 45 days of grief. Each day is written like a journal entry where you will get glimpses of my story as I describe my feelings, but it may appear sporadic and non-sequential. If you are interested in the details of my full story, my autobiography is published on Amazon and Audible and titled *Mentally STRONG: Against all Odds*.

Professionally, I have been a psychiatric nurse practitioner since 2000, and have gained extensive experience over the last several decades. My medical career began as an Army Medic before attending nursing school and receiving a master's degree as a Psychiatric Nurse Practitioner at Florida International University (FIU). I next went on to receive a doctorate in Education at Nova Southeastern University. As a result of my own personal struggles, I developed the Mentally STRONG Method to help myself and others gain mental strength and move forward despite setbacks. In 2018, I founded the first Mentally STRONG Clinic in Colorado Springs, CO. where I still practice today.

This workbook will incorporate many of the methods we use at the clinic and will help you take control of your own grief as I have similarly done after experiencing the loss of three of my children. No matter what your personal situation, I'm certain that this workbook can assist you with processing the grief you're experiencing. I hope that hearing my story and sharing my grief journey will serve as an inspiration. Please know that I've felt what you are feeling and have been where you are. As a result, I feel confident in the knowledge that Controlled Grief, and the Mentally STRONG Method, can help you process your emotions in a way that will enable you to move forward while still honoring your loved one.

What is Controlled Grief?

Controlled Grief is grieving in a way that is more deliberate than what you may normally think of as grieving. In fact, it is the conscious act of taking control of the grieving process. It is not wallowing in sorrow or spending days on end feeling sorry for yourself. Instead, it involves setting aside certain blocks of time to engage in activities that help you process your loss and work through your emotions. There is no one right way to grieve and you may find that your timeline and schedule look different than someone else who has experienced a similar loss (that's okay and to be expected).

Anyone who tells you that you should get on with life and get over your loss according to a specific timeline is doing you a disservice. Your grief journey is your own, and by practicing Controlled Grief you can process your emotions while still engaging in everyday activities.

Who Should Use This Guidebook?

This workbook was written for anyone who has experienced a significant loss. Whether your loss occurred yesterday or many years ago, you can still benefit from actively grieving and following the steps and activities outlined in this workbook.

Go At Your Own Pace

Although I chose to grieve in a consecutive 45-day window, you may choose a different timeline. It's really up to you and your preferences and schedule. I encourage you to choose a number of days that means something to you personally (45 has always been a meaningful number to my family) and embark on them consecutively. This initial experience will jumpstart your lifelong journey. The whole point of this process is that grieving is important. So, know that you can do it in a way that best works for you (while still following this 45-day outline). I initially chose to grieve in the morning, but later decided to engage in the grieving process throughout the day or in the evenings. You may decide to participate in these activities in the morning, evening, or afternoon. There is no right or wrong time and schedule. Pick a pace that you are comfortable with and that gives you the most benefit in terms of the process.

You can also follow my 45 days of grief by watching my documentary on my YouTube Channel: youtube.com/drbmentallystrong

Start Where You Are (Your Feelings and Thoughts)

Just as each of us has a different grief experience, we are all also starting from a different place. Perhaps you are new to your loss, or maybe you have been carrying your loss for many years. No matter when that starting point was, you have to begin this Controlled Grief process where you are. Think about or journal the answers to the following questions in preparation for your grief journey:

- What grief experience are you processing?

- Have you experienced other types of grief or losses in the past?

- Who has or will support you?

- What are you currently feeling about this loss?

- How do you feel about embarking on this Controlled Grief process?

- What are your goals at the end of these 45 days?

- How can you circumvent any obstacles?

- What is your truth? What do you no longer believe to be true?

How to Use This Guidebook

Each day, allot the time needed for your Controlled Grief activity and nurturing your 5 Self's. The order and timeframe should be intuitive (and not set in stone). You will have many opportunities to read my 45-day journey, seeing both my pain and my breakthroughs. As I was working through my 45 days of grief, I created several Choice Opportunities that I found helpful during my journey (I've shared them with you throughout this workbook). Each day, you will have a journal prompt for the following elements and a Choice Opportunity to complete.

Controlled Grief: An activity, action, or thought that brings up memories of your loved one, for the purpose of evoking emotions. It involves a conscious effort to feel the pain. If we learn to feel the pain in a healthy manner, the intensity and frequency of that pain will decrease. Examples include but are not limited to looking at pictures of your loved one, talking with a friend about a memory, or going through their things.

The 5 Self's

- **Spiritual Self:** We are physical, mental, emotional, and spiritual beings. During this process, I challenge you to develop your Spiritual Self. This is not a proselytization or evangelical activity. This is specific to you and your relationship with the spiritual world. There are many readers that do not believe in one source or being that I may call God. Growing and nurturing your Spiritual Self, however, is beyond your belief system. If you have a spiritual belief system, then you'll begin this activity with that belief system in mind. The challenge for you will be to grow, connect, and receive. If you do not have a spiritual belief system or get angered by the thought of turning to a spiritual source for strength and growth, I challenge you to learn to meditate. In this book, I discuss several modalities that I used for spiritual connection and meditation, but this is your journey. I often talk about my relationship with God because I want to be authentic in what I am sharing in this book. A relationship with God is authentic to me but could be different for you.

- **Self-Regulation:** Self-Regulation is the ability to control your emotions and responses. I often refer to the Mentally STRONG Method as a tool for being able to self-regulate. Many of you have great coping and self-regulation skills that you have been using during your grieving. In this book, you will see several examples of my self-regulation skills too. They include being able to continue working and doing what I'm passionate about while grieving the loss of my children. Each day, you will be prompted to write how you self-regulated the emotions that are being brought up by doing this Controlled Grief.

- **Self-Movement:** We don't often think about movement in processing grief, but trauma, pain, and processing are actual movements. Many people talk about the importance of processing emotions but don't teach you how to do it. You can process emotions by moving them out of the body. Sometimes that is a physical movement like going for a walk. When I got angry during this process, I hit a punching bag. That is a physical movement to release anger from the body. It can also be a subtle movement like the vibration of music. It could be watching the movement of a fire, feeling the wind and sand on your feet, or allowing the ocean waves to roll past your ankles. I want you to find a movement that works for you, so you feel like you're moving the grief out of your body. Go slowly. Each movement might transfer a little bit of the pain, but maybe not move it completely out of the body. What we hold on to will impact us forever, so allow the pain of grief to be moved in whatever way you can think of. It can be obvious and physical (like going for a run), or any kind of creative movement (painting, dancing, etc.).

- **Self-Improvement:** Each day, you will be challenged to learn something new. During my 45 days of grief, I researched various grief theories and read several books. The purpose of having Self-Improvement in the Five Self's is that if we can improve ourselves, we can move forward and find purpose in our lives. I believe in continuous self-improvement as a lifelong learner and feel that it is even more important with intense grief because it's easy to become stagnant and feel like there's nothing worth learning anymore. In my journey, I studied grief, but you can choose to learn anything you want in your own Self-Improvement journey. Perhaps you might learn a new coping skill or a different hobby that you enjoy doing. The choice is yours.

- **Self-Care:** We must not forget Self-Care. For some of you, that involves the basics like getting a decent night's sleep, eating foods that are good for you, and making choices to care for yourself day-to-day. When you're experiencing intense grief or any kind of deep pain, self-care is often one of the first things that you stop doing. During your journey, I challenge you to find something to do to take care of yourself every day. Some days, that might be taking a short nap, sleeping in, or allowing yourself to have a milkshake. On other days, you will be challenged to take care of things that you've ignored for a long time (like I did). Maybe you haven't been to the dentist in years or perhaps there is something more serious that you never followed up on. Now is the time to do so.

The 45 Day Journey

Day 1 - Dr. B's Experience

Theme: Embarking on the journey.
Mood: Feeling off.

On day one, I was feeling anxious and apprehensive, not so much about participating, but more about whether it would help or prove to be insightful. I just wasn't sure if something would come out of it. The thought of embarking on a 45- day journey was a little overwhelming, even for a mental health professional like me. But at the end of the day, I truly wanted to dedicate the time to grieving and to processing my emotions in a way that I hadn't been able to before. I knew that I needed to do it, but it was already exhausting on the first day. My mom told me 45 days was a long time and I began to believe that she was right.

I started the morning with meditation, creating an environment where I could really focus and have things available to help me pray and meditate. Sometimes tools can be helpful, like cards or prayer beads. I fumbled around with those things and asked myself, how can I get into the mindset of prayer and meditation? Honestly, I have so much anger towards God and have trouble trusting Him and my intuition. I am also reluctant to trust my positive thoughts.

I feel like so much has been taken away from me. Meditation and prayer are about connecting, but my mind was distracted by the noises upstairs. I want to believe that my children are in a beautiful place of love and contentment, but it is a struggle at times. My logical brain goes back and forth, and meditation and prayer are not about our logical brain.

As I was sitting there trying to meditate, I got a whisper in my ear from my late 21-year-old daughter Miah. "Don't forget what I've told you. Don't forget what I've told you." I've had experiences where Miah said to me, "time and space are human limitations, but I am right here next to you." I envisioned her leaning her head on my shoulder. Even though, in life, she was taller than me, she was still my little girl who would stand next to me with her arms around me. I felt her, but it didn't seem like enough.

It often feels easier to push through the pain than to actually sit with it. I worry that if I sit with my pain, I will become depressed and not be able to get myself out of it.

I always felt that if I was good enough, that God was going to rescue me and care for me. So, I focused on saving my kids and was in fight or flight mode for 15 years. I believed that if I was smart enough, I would've found the right treatment for them, but I never did. At the end of it, I felt like I missed something. Even on the day of Reggie's death, I missed the physical signs. He was not breathing well, and I didn't react quickly enough. I was mad at myself then and still am now to some extent.

After Reggie passed away, I told God that I wasn't going to let it happen again. I said that I didn't care if Miah only had a minor cold, I was taking her to the emergency room. I didn't want to miss anything else. And then she died in her sleep. There was nothing to miss, except maybe I should have been sleeping next to her.

After some time in meditation, I decided that I would start my Controlled Grief process and began to go through a box of toys. As I shuffled through them, I realized that I had so many of Miah's toys but didn't really have a lot of Reggie's toys because he was already sick when we moved to Colorado. There were lots of Build-a-Bears. That was Miah's thing. I picked up one from when she was a cheerleader. It was a little dirty, and definitely one of her older bears, but I decided to put it on display. It brought back many warm memories and made me miss her even more.

Later, I dug into some grief research regarding the 5 Stages of Grief: denial, bargaining, depression, anger, and acceptance. The denial stage really stood out to me. If you linger in the denial stage, you're going to have physical symptoms around that. For me, today, those symptoms were coming out in irritability. When I was working through the anger, bargaining, and depression stages, I concluded that those three are all enmeshed together for me. And, as I talk about in the Mentally STRONG Method, things need to be organized and dealt with differently. I wonder if I can take my anger and anxiety and move it. I wonder if I can give it less energy and intensity. That would be beneficial in many ways.

Bargaining after a major loss, like losing a child, is really about struggling with the purpose. You wonder *why me*? Just the word *"why"* brings an emotional energy. But the reality is that we don't get to know why. We can try to make a purpose for it, but we aren't given the reason and we have to make peace with that. I wrapped up day one with these thoughts on my mind, knowing that I had experienced all five stages of grief, yet was still entrenched in some of them.

Dr. B's Controlled Grief and 5 SELF's Process Day 1

Controlled Grief: I allotted time and allowed my emotions to come to the surface while I looked through Miah's toys.

- o **Spiritual Self:** As I meditated, I was reminded of previous experiences with Reggie and Miah. I acknowledged my eternal relationship with them.
- o **Self-Improvement:** I studied The 5 Stages of Grief.
- o **Self-Movement:** I walked on the treadmill, trying to release anger and irritability.
- o **Self-Regulation/Choose:** I listened to an academic podcast to regulate my emotional response and chose to prepare for giving a presentation.
- o **Self-Care:** I got a massage.

My Controlled Grief Journey Day 1

Date: / /

What is your mood today?

(circle or fill in your own word)

Open	Loving	Sad	Guilty
Calm	Present	Depressed	Afraid
Relaxed	Safe	Broken Hearted	Overwhelmed
Hopeful	Angry	Irritable	Exhausted
Connected	Furious	Longing	Drained
Strong	Resentful	Disconnected	Numb

What activity did you choose to practice for **Controlled Grief**? _____

_____

What have you done today to empower your **Spiritual Self**? _____

_____

How did you practice **Self-Regulation** today? _____

_____

How were you able to work on **Self-Improvement** today? _____

_____

How were you able to prioritize your **Self-Care**? _____

_____

How were you able to work on **Self-Movement** today? _____

_____

Any other thoughts you want to remember about your **journey** today?

_____

Choice Opportunity of the Day

I chose *Controlled Grief* as the first Choice Opportunity because I have been doing this for myself over the last five years (since 2016 when my son died). Beginning to grieve is a conscious choice, and this activity reminds you that you have control of that grief (a vital concept to understand throughout this process). Learning about control is important and that's why you are doing this Choice Opportunity on Day 1. This is your first step in the 45 days of grief! Good luck.

Choice Opportunity: Controlled Grief

Expected outcome: Understand the nature of grief and the use of "controlled grief" to maintain a purpose and level of functioning in the midst of intense emotional and disabling pain from a significant loss experienced.

What is the grief process? Often, those who are grieving a loss are taught that grief is a process that ends in acceptance of the loss and are told to move on or to get over the loss: to accept it.

This is not accurate. Grief is painful. Grief is a loss that deserves recognition, processing, and time. From the experiences of many, trying to obtain this end goal of "acceptance" only leads to artificially accepting the loss which only suppresses the painful and intense feelings from the loss. This is why unsurmountable grief can arise and interfere with future decision making and interfere with your personal vision.

It is important to acknowledge that your loss and grief are not in line with what you want in your life and that this loss is the opposite of your personal vision. I cannot stress the importance of devoting time to grieving but to not let it be consuming for a long period of time. This is where controlled grief is instrumental as a tool to manage and process the grief. If you let the grief be overwhelmingly impactful in your life, you are missing out on life, but more importantly, you are creating negative pathways of thinking in your brain. This negative pathway over time becomes more difficult to reverse and overcome: not impossible, just more difficult

Step 1: From your Thought Map list the grief that you have identified and the need you are facing with the loss: recent grief, delayed grief, anticipatory grief.

1. _____

2. _____

3. _____

4. _____

5. _____

Learn more about *The Mentally STRONG Method*: 1-800-55-STRONG ~ www.mentallystrong.com

*The Mentally STRONG Method with Choice Opportunities© Author: Cristi Bundukamara – not for reproduction/distribution

Step 2: Follow the doctor orders in the Controlled Grief prescription: Appropriate processing of grief over time with the use of controlled grief should result in a decrease intensity of the feelings from grief and lower frequency with which the grief affects you.

- Identify the grief affecting your mood. Sit with a picture, memorabilia, or cherished item from your loved one/loss you experienced. Feel the pain of your loss with intention to remember and honor the loss.
- Feel the range of feelings. Be sure to express your thoughts and talk to the person or the loss. Get your thoughts out with honesty and clarity.
- PRN: when intense or unexpected memories emerge with triggers, take time for controlled grief, then return to your normal activities.
- On special occasions or anniversary, take the whole day off.

Step 3: Create a plan for controlled grief as ordered. Set aside the time for yourself and allow yourself to grieve. Outline your plan:

_____

_____

- Suppressing grief for long periods of time is not effective or healthy.
- Suppressing your grief until after work might be appropriate.
- Grief is not about acceptance. You will always feel the loss.

There will be pain and other feelings. However, in time, the frequency and intensity of your grief will decrease.

This is your Choice Opportunity to be   Mentally STRONG   in grief.

Learn more about *The Mentally STRONG Method*: 1-800-55-STRONG ~ www.mentallystrong.com

Day 2- Dr. B's Experience

Theme: Grace with yourself and patience with the process. Emotional pain is exhausting; you can't do all the work in one day.
Mood: Hopelessness and the need for movement.

I felt overwhelmed and sad in the morning, unable to get out of bed. I experienced immense pain while looking through pictures of my children. During my morning meditation, I had lots of questions around Reggie and Miah's deaths. I lit a purple candle for Miah and a red candle for Reggie. I decided the focus of my meditation would be asking God the questions that I had for Him. That's what meditation is supposed to be, a place where you can ask and receive. Why did Miah and Reggie have to die? What was the greater purpose? Why did Miah die so suddenly? Why me? Why pain in the world at all?

I didn't find the meditation helpful. It triggered hopeless feelings and I decided to give up before I was able to fully connect. I pondered whether or not I wanted to get up and take a shower, but I chose to grieve instead. I grieved for a long time until I felt like there were no more tears left. Wiping my face, I came to the conclusion that I likely needed to do my Controlled Grief in the evenings because I have an obligation to work, but I committed to it for that morning.

I chose to pick up the stuffed animals again and the grief at the sight of them was overwhelming. I would bring Miah a stuffed animal every time I came back from a Navy trip. I embraced one for a long time and was happy to hold something that was once held by my child. I wrapped up my Controlled Grief session on that note and concluded that I had made some progress that morning.

At work today, I engaged in a Narrative Exposure Therapy session with one of the Nurse Practitioners at Mentally STRONG, Angel. We established a visual timeline of my life. The purpose of the Narrative Exposure Therapy was to identify any traumas in my timeline (or story) and to treat them using a technique called Brain Spotting in a future session.

On this day, I experienced a lot of ups and downs, and had to remind myself that it can't all be done at once. Grieving takes time. I engaged in Self-Care by having an

Journal

Use this page to journal any thoughts and feelings you may be experiencing along your journey:

_____

_____

_____

_____

_____

_____

_____

_____

_____

_____

_____

_____

_____

_____

_____

_____

_____

_____

_____

_____

_____

_____

outdoor lunch with my sister at the beautiful Garden of the Gods, reflecting upon the day. I felt that, once again, I had made progress, letting go of some of the things that I can't control and acknowledging the enormous stress that I'd been through. I still had many days ahead of me to accomplish even more during these 45 days.

Dr. B's Controlled Grief and 5 SELF's Process Day 2

Controlled Grief: I looked at pictures of my children.

- o **Spiritual Self:** I continued to meditate on trying to get answers to the questions related to my losses.
- o **Self-Improvement:** I studied dialectical thinking in grief.
- o **Self-Movement:** I walked on the treadmill, attempting to move the pain.
- o **Self-Regulation/Choose:** I chose to get moving and do something productive. I reminded myself that it can't all be done at one time.
- o **Self-Care:** I went to an outdoor lunch with my sister.

My Controlled Grief Journey Day 2

Date: /   /

What is your mood today?
(circle or fill in your own word)

Open	Loving	Sad	Guilty
Calm	Present	Depressed	Afraid
Relaxed	Safe	Broken Hearted	Overwhelmed
Hopeful	Angry	Irritable	Exhausted
Connected	Furious	Longing	Drained
Strong	Resentful	Disconnected	Numb

What activity did you choose to practice for **Controlled Grief**? _____

_____

What have you done today to empower your **Spiritual Self**? _____

_____

How did you practice **Self-Regulation** today? _____

_____

How were you able to work on **Self-Improvement** today? _____

_____

How were you able to prioritize your **Self-Care**? _____

_____

How were you able to work on **Self-Movement** today? _____

_____

Any other thoughts you want to remember about your **journey** today?

_____

Choice Opportunity of the day:

The Choice Opportunity that I chose for Day 2 is *Acknowledging Grief*. It is based on the grief theory that many of us learn in school (denial, avoidance, anger, questioning, and depression). Intense grief is so messy that this basic theory seems almost elementary compared to my pain, but it is a good place to start in terms of understanding what theorists say about the grief process.

Choice Opportunity: Acknowledging Grief

Grief is a deep emotional response to a great loss. Grief is the process that ultimately brings healing through the pain. Working through the pain may move through different stages. Identifying the different stages can give you some knowledge about the grief process. Remember that grief is unique to each person. Be patient and compassionate with yourself.

Stages of Grief	What it can look like	What it can feel like	Thoughts you may have
Denial	Avoidance procrastination forgetting easily distracted mindless behavior keeping busy all the time	shock numbness confusion shutting down	This can't be happening. Thinking/saying: I'm fine or It's fine.
Avoidance	running away increased alcohol or drug use jumping into another relationship staying busy isolating	overwhelmed withdrawn fragile empty	I don't want to think about it.
Anger	pessimism sarcasm irritability getting into arguments physical fights	frustration impatience resentment embarrassment rage	Why is this happening to me?
Questioning (Bargaining)	over-thinking and worrying predicting the future and assuming the worst	guilt shame fear anxiety insecurity blame	I will do anything to change this. I should have . . . If only . . .
Depression	sleep and appetitie changes reduced energy reduced social interests reduced motivation crying	sadness helplessness hopelessness disappointment despair	What's the point of going on after this loss?
Be Present (Acceptance)	acknowledge the reality of the loss being present in the moment adapting coping	courageous wisdom hopeful sorrow and joy peace	After this loss, my world is so different. It may not be easy but it is possible.

This is your Choice Opportunity to be Mentally STRONG®

Learn more about *The Mentally STRONG Method:* 1-800-55-STRONG ~ www.mentallystrong.com

*The Mentally STRONG Method with Choice Opportunities©Author: Cristi Bundukamara – not for reproduction/distribution

Choice Opportunity: Acknowledging Grief

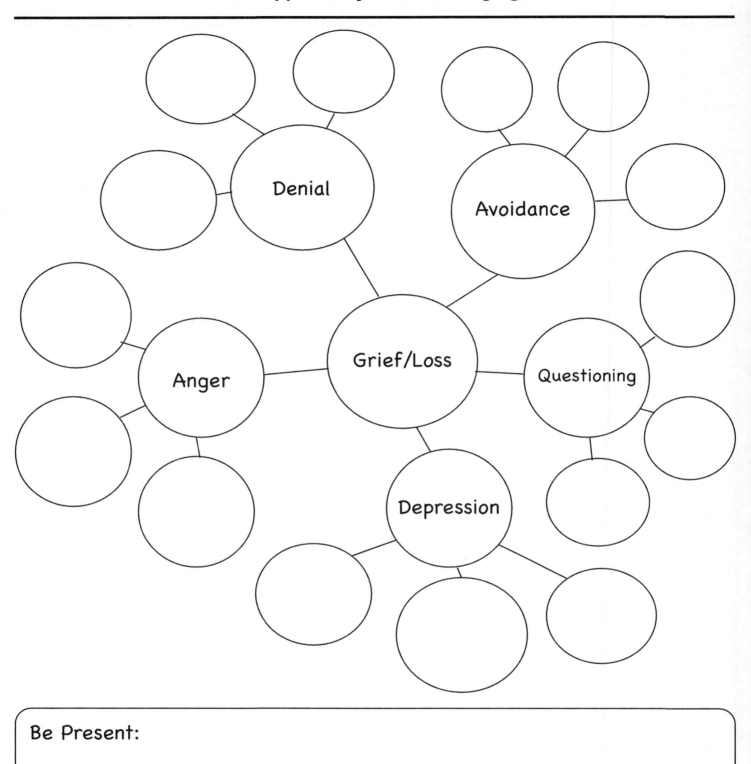

Denial

Avoidance

Grief/Loss

Anger

Questioning

Depression

Be Present:

This is your Choice Opportunity to be  Mentally STRONG®

Learn more about *The Mentally STRONG Method*: 1-800-55-STRONG ~ www.mentallystrong.com

*The Mentally STRONG Method with Choice Opportunities©Author: Cristi Bundukamara – not for reproduction/distribution

Day 3 - Dr. B's Experience

Theme: Spiritual connection.
Mood: Can-do attitude.

I began this day by meditating on my Personal Vision: to have a genuine relationship with God. Some of the barriers that I identified were things that I was taught growing up. I'd often wondered why hardship was allowed and why my prayers went unanswered. Searching, I reflected upon several Bible passages.

It was a travel day as I'd decided to go to Dallas to get a SPECT scan (a noninvasive nuclear imaging test) as a type of Self-Care and to measure the changes in my brain over the 45 days of grief. While I was there, as a form of Controlled Grief, I recalled moments related to the last time that I was in Dallas for Reggie's DBS Brain Surgery at Cook Children's Hospital and how a well-known pastor prayed over the whole family. That had been a time of hopefulness and believing that we might have found something that could help. It was traumatic to contrast where I was then (hopeful and fighting) to where I am now, sitting in the tremendous pain of grief.

Once at the Amen clinic, the tech explained to me that they give a computer test to stimulate the brain and inject a tracer for the images. He said, "While you're taking the test and your brain's active, I come in and do the injection. There are no side effects at all. It just lets us see the brain. Once you finish, we go straight over to the machine and take the scan." It was as he said, and the scan proceeded without complication. I was interested, yet a little apprehensive to see the results. Still, I felt empowered by flying to Dallas and engaging in this test as a form of self-care and measurement. After the scan concluded, I flew back home. It was a busy day travelling alone which left plenty of time for reflection.

On Day 3, I had a "I can do this" attitude and high expectations of myself. I tried to conceptualize how I self-regulate so that I could communicate it to others. I concluded that doing a SPECT scan was a powerful choice of self-care for myself, and I was proud of my choices and progress that day.

"Embrace
the
Journey"
~ Dr. B

Journal

Use this page to journal any thoughts and feelings you may be experiencing along your journey:

_____

_____

_____

_____

_____

_____

_____

_____

_____

_____

_____

_____

_____

_____

_____

_____

_____

_____

_____

_____

_____

Dr. B's Controlled Grief and 5 SELF's Process Day 3

Controlled Grief: I spent time remembering the last time I was in Dallas was for Reggie's DBS Brain Surgery at Cook Children's Hospital.

- o **Spiritual Self**: I meditated on my Personal Vision: to have a genuine relationship with God.
- o **Self-Improvement:** I studied Moving Through Grief based on ACT.
- o **Self-Movement**: I engaged in physical travel.
- o **Self-Regulation/Choose**: I had an attitude of I can do it!
- o **Self-Care**: I decided to do the Amen assessment and SPECT scan as a form of self-care (and to measure changes in my brain).

My Controlled Grief Journey Day 3   Date: /   /

What is your mood today?
(circle or fill in your own word)

Open	Loving	Sad	Guilty
Calm	Present	Depressed	Afraid
Relaxed	Safe	Broken Hearted	Overwhelmed
Hopeful	Angry	Irritable	Exhausted
Connected	Furious	Longing	Drained
Strong	Resentful	Disconnected	Numb

What activity did you choose to practice for **Controlled Grief**? _____

_____

What have you done today to empower your **Spiritual Self**? _____

_____

How did you practice **Self-Regulation** today? _____

_____

How were you able to work on **Self-Improvement** today? _____

_____

How were you able to prioritize your **Self-Care**? _____

_____

How were you able to work on **Self-Movement** today? _____

_____

Any other thoughts you want to remember about your **journey** today?

_____

Choice Opportunity of the day:
Day 3 is one of three times that I'll ask you to use a grief theory to process your grief. So, for today, use the *Process Using Grief Theories* Choice Opportunity. Identify what you can relate to from the grief theory you choose, or what helps you, as well as what does not resonate with you or doesn't help you.

Choice Opportunity: Process using Grief Theories

Use the Mentally STRONG Grief series or an internet search. Choose one or more grief theories. Study and/or meditate on the concepts of the grief theory.

Sample list of grief theories to get you started, various theorists:

- 5 Stages of Grief
- Dialectical Thinking in Grief
- Moving Through Grief
- Grow Around Your Grief
- 4 Tasks of Grief
- Physical Impact of Grief
- The 6 R's of Mourning

- The Dual Process Model of Grief
- Grief Work Theory
- The Grieving Brain
- Grief and Attachment
- Continuing Bonds
- Trajectories of Grief
- Find your own

In your own words, describe the grief theory that you chose:

_____

_____

_____

_____

Acknowledge any triggers or negative responses. For example, "that's not how I feel", "it's not that easy", or "I can never accept this".

_____

_____

_____

_____

Now reframe or minimize the above negative statements. For example: "Acceptance doesn't have to mean it's okay, it can be an acknowledgement of the pain, even if that pain is there for the rest of your life." Write your reframed positive statement below:

_____

_____

_____

Learn more about *The Mentally STRONG Method*: **1-800-55-STRONG ~ www.mentallystrong.com**

What did you learn from this grief theory?

_____

_____

_____

_____

Based on your personal grief journey, what criticisms do you have of this grief theory?

_____

_____

_____

_____

What is your personal take away from studying this grief theory? For example: coping strategies, interventions, change in mindset, or grace given to yourself.

_____

_____

_____

_____

This is your Choice Opportunity to be Mentally STRONG® in learning about grief.

Learn more about *The Mentally STRONG Method*: 1-800-55-STRONG ~ www.mentallystrong.com

*The Mentally STRONG Method with Choice Opportunities© Author: Cristi Bundukamara – not for reproduction/distribution

Day 4 – Dr. B's Experience

Theme: Sleep as Self-Care.
Mood: Seeking connection and care.

I allowed myself to sleep in today as a form of self-care and love. When I got up, I decided that I was going to meditate on something that I had just learned: that I would like to receive. I wanted to use some meditation tools to help me focus. I've received a few spiritual messages from my children and one of the books I've read was about mediumship and people who've had spiritual experiences. Unfortunately, I tend to get so afraid in this space, not of the reality, but of what others will think.

During my morning meditation session, I discovered that things often distract me from being present but decided that I want to actually own and meditate on those things. I'd asked my husband to turn down the TV and be quiet so that I could meditate. When he started moving around upstairs, I became annoyed. I was trying to ignore it and be present and ready to receive, but part of that receiving is acknowledging the reality that my husband is here. And acknowledging that, although we have a hard time grieving together, this is our shared grief. We have lost our children as a couple.

It was also my first time using a sound bowl. A sound bowl is an auditory tool to help with focus and it worked for me. While using it, I asked to hear from Reggie and Miah. Miah felt the closest. I heard her say, "I'm right here, Mommy." Even though I was overjoyed at the connection, I wondered why hearing from her is often not enough for me.

My thoughts turned towards Reggie and Johnny. Were they here too? I often talk about the fact that the way to process things is through movement and getting it out of the body. That movement can be through Self-Improvement, sounds, or energetic work. Unfortunately, I hadn't had a chance to participate in any physical movement yet that morning.

I was about to end my meditation but decided that I still wanted to move something. The tuning fork can be used for movement (vibrations), so I picked it up. I just didn't know what I wanted to move. I thought about what it could be. Maybe I wanted to move my fear of being honest about my journey and spiritual walk. Perhaps it was about moving out my fear related to using spiritual tools. Although I do believe in God, I also think that they are just a fraction of what God can represent, and what we as humans can experience spiritually. As a grieving mother, I want to investigate all aspects of this spirituality and intuition and try to connect with my children using some methods that may be frowned upon by the church. Even so, there's this real fear there in terms of communicating what I'm experiencing (and the judgement that I might receive as a result).

At the end of the session, my heart was still broken, but it did feel like I'd experienced a clearance, and that empowered me. I was set up for the day, which was great because I had a morning of meetings followed by a professional conference in the afternoon.

By the end of my day (7:45 PM), I still hadn't had the chance to do any Controlled Grief and was feeling a little overwhelmed with the whole process. So, I looked at pictures of Miah, Reggie, and Johnny and reflected upon our relationships and time together here on earth. I found one of Reggie and Grandma, and then another of Miah the same year, and some others where we were all vacationing together. I kept flipping through the pictures until I came to another of Miah which haunted me. She was lying in the same position that I found her in when she passed away - on top of the pillows - and looking so happy.

There were still more from parties and trips and one where we were at the beach house. Miah was wearing a mermaid tail. How she loved mermaids and the swimming pool. Then I realized how much she looked like me in that picture. There were few of Johnny though because he was only with us for a year.

Looking over all of the pictures, my heart filled with love, and I acknowledged how much I'd fought for my children. There were so many great memories that we shared. My eyelids began to get heavy, so on that note, I allowed myself to go to bed early in line with my own self-care and love.

Dr. B's Controlled Grief and 5 SELF's Process Day 4

Controlled Grief: I looked through pictures of my children.

- o **Spiritual Self**: I asked to hear from Reggie and Miah.
- o **Self-Improvement:** I read the book: *Don't Kiss Them Goodbye*. I also researched the use of a Medium to communicate with your loved one.
- o **Self-Movement**: The vibration of a tuning fork.
- o **Self-Regulation/Choose**: I chose to sit with feeling the pain until the intensity of my emotions subsided.
- o **Self-Care:** I allowed myself to sleep in and to go to bed early.

My Controlled Grief Journey Day 4

Date: / /

What is your mood today?
(circle or fill in your own word)

Open	Loving	Sad	Guilty
Calm	Present	Depressed	Afraid
Relaxed	Safe	Broken Hearted	Overwhelmed
Hopeful	Angry	Irritable	Exhausted
Connected	Furious	Longing	Drained
Strong	Resentful	Disconnected	Numb

What activity did you choose to practice for **Controlled Grief**? _____

_____

What have you done today to empower your **Spiritual Self**? _____

_____

How did you practice **Self-Regulation** today? _____

_____

How were you able to work on **Self-Improvement** today? _____

_____

How were you able to prioritize your **Self-Care**? _____

_____

How were you able to work on **Self-Movement** today? _____

_____

Any other thoughts you want to remember about your **journey** today?

_____

Choice Opportunity of the day:

When you have experienced intense grief, you often wonder why it's happened to you or why you have to go through so much pain. That's why I chose the Choice Opportunity of *Why Me* for you to complete on Day 4.

Choice Opportunity: Why Me?

Expected Outcome: Gain insight into and reframe the "Why me?" question and create a new, more realistic statement.

Step # 1: Think about and describe three logical reasons that "Why me?" is not a fair question

_____

_____

_____

Step #2 What is your current thought behind the "Why me?" question? Circle all that apply:

Aggravated	Embarrassed	Powerless
Afraid	Empty	Rejected
Alienated	Envious	Sad
Angry	Exhausted	Scared
Annoyed	Fearful	Sensitive
Anxious	Frustrated	Skeptical
Ashamed	Grief	Shocked
Awful	Guilty	Stressed
Chaotic	Heartbroken	Suspicious
Confused	Hurt	Terrified
Crushed	Ignored	Threatened
Depressed	Inadequate	Vulnerable
Devastated	Irritated	Worried
Disappointed	Jealous	Worthless
Drained	Lonely	Withdrawn
Disgusted	Overwhelmed	

Learn more about _The Mentally STRONG Method_: 1-800-55-STRONG ~ www.mentallystrong.com

*The Mentally STRONG Method with Choice Opportunities© Author: Cristi Bundukamara – not for reproduction/distribution

Step #3 Make a list of the factors that you CANNOT change

_____

_____

_____

_____

Step #4 Make a list of the factors that I CAN Change

_____

_____

_____

_____

Step #5 Write a new, realistic statement that counteracts the question "Why me?"

_____

_____

_____

This is your _Choice Opportunity_ to be   Mentally STRONG™ and reframe!

Learn more about _The Mentally STRONG Method_: 1-800-55-STRONG ~ www.mentallystrong.com

Day 5 – Dr. B's Experience

Theme: Coming together through grief.
Mood: Optimistic and believing in myself.

During my morning meditation, I used tarot cards as a tool. I've been using them to just kind of connect spiritually and for active meditation. I know that these cards can have a negative connotation, but I do think that God has used them. Still, I get a little scared because I was saved in a very conservative church that would say that these cards are evil.

All that I can tell you is that using them is helping me and doesn't negate what I believe about God. It has just given me a tool to ask questions. So, I wrote down some questions for the session. The first one was: Why? Sometimes I think I know why. Still, I don't know how to nurture and trust my intuition because it has been wrong in the past. I'd truly believed that Reggie would be healed even though repeatedly there were signs showing me that it probably wouldn't happen. I held on to hope for a very long time. I believed that Miah would live for at least 10 more years. Neither of those beliefs turned out to be true.

The next question I had was: Can I trust? Trust this path that I'm going on? And that was my meditation. I used the cards as collective energy, collective knowledge, and to ask questions to God about the divine and about everything that's so complicated for my human mind to grasp. So, I decided to do a three-card spread of what's conscious, what's unconscious, and maybe get some kind of advice.

My next questions were: Can I trust my intuition? What is conscious? The King of Swords is conscious. With my rational brain, things have to make sense. I want them to make sense of it. But what is the unconscious? Queen of Cups. Consciously, I want to be an organized leader. And unconsciously, I'm an emotional queen. Maybe it's not so unconsciously. I know that's who I am. I'm loving and kind, and that's my intention. My advice is the seven of wands. That consciousness is challenged. I have to fight for my truth, defend my beliefs, and protect my position. I don't like conflict though. Then I heard God say, "It's not conflict, it is love." It is how you feel. My love, conscious, and unconscious advice. It's even defending those emotions. We're taught that emotions cannot be trusted. In one of the grief books that I read yesterday; it said that emotions are not facts. They're just information. But they're facts for me.

Still, my pain is real, and I'm being challenged to fight for that. I've always felt God or experienced God like a king of swords, or a rational ruler. But when I look at my life, and when I listen to the stories of my patients' lives, with all the trauma that people have experienced and the evil in the world, it doesn't feel very just.

You are not simple, God. You are more complex than our human brains can comprehend. I decided that I would be true to myself. Throughout this process, I received confirmation that my heart is kind and loving and that I am supposed to share my experiences. It gave validation to my entire grief journey and plan to share my experiences with others.

Later, I moved Miah's and Reggie's ashes as my Controlled Grief experience. We planted a tree with Johnny's ashes, so I don't still have them physically with me. This was actually a combination of Controlled Grief and movement. I knew that it would be very hard, but I had made up my mind. I wanted to display the ashes on a shelf, so I brought them down from where they were by the front door. I'd originally thought that having them there would remind me of them every time I walked out the door. But the truth is that I don't go out the front door very often, so they needed a better spot.

Moving the ashes caused me to remember the time when, just after Reggie died, I went to the funeral home to pick his ashes up. I went alone because I thought I could manage it. I'd walked in and signed for them, with lots of people around me telling me they were sorry for my loss. When I'd gotten to my car, I'd just kind of stared down at them. They were in a cardboard box with Reggie's name scribbled on it. That's when I realized that was all that was left of him. That was it! That's all I had. Me, his mother, who loved him more than life. I sat in that car for what seemed like an eternity and wept until I ran out of tears. I didn't know if I could go on. How could I go on? The intensity of the day was something that I will never forget. The pain and sorrow during that moment and many moments since were unbearable. Moving the ashes brought all of that back up for me. Once more I wept and wept. Were these ashes all that I had left? How could that be?

I allowed myself to cry on and off throughout the day, taking lots of deep breaths and remaining as present as I could. I made peace with the process. I allowed my emotions to go up and down naturally, leaning into my sorrow at times and then coming out of it.

Later, I reflected upon my grief. I decided that even though I'd felt a lot of pain and cried a good deal, it was very healing for me to get it out. I concluded that I was good with where I was and didn't need to self-regulate. I'd learned a lot this day in terms of trusting myself and the process.

Dr. B's Controlled Grief and 5 SELF's Process Day 5

Controlled Grief: I moved Miah and Reggie's ashes.

- o **Spiritual Self**: I used tarot as a spiritual tool.
- o **Self-Improvement**: I read Dr. Lois Tonkin's *Growing Around Grief.*
- o **Self-Movement**: I walked on my treadmill while doing Controlled Grief.
- o **Self-Regulation/Choose**: I felt pretty good today and didn't need to self-regulate.
- o **Self-Care:** I focused on loving food that loves me back.

My Controlled Grief Journey Day 5   Date: /   /

What is your mood today?
(circle or fill in your own word)

Open	Loving	Sad	Guilty
Calm	Present	Depressed	Afraid
Relaxed	Safe	Broken Hearted	Overwhelmed
Hopeful	Angry	Irritable	Exhausted
Connected	Furious	Longing	Drained
Strong	Resentful	Disconnected	Numb

What activity did you choose to practice for **Controlled Grief**? _____

_____

What have you done today to empower your **Spiritual Self**? _____

_____

How did you practice **Self-Regulation** today? _____

_____

How were you able to work on **Self-Improvement** today? _____

_____

How were you able to prioritize your **Self-Care**? _____

_____

How were you able to work on **Self-Movement** today? _____

_____

Any other thoughts you want to remember about your **journey** today?

_____

Choice Opportunity of the day:

For Day 5, I chose *Your Grief Ritual* as your Choice Opportunity. Many grief theories talk about having a grief ritual that gives you pleasure and joy. For me, that grief ritual is sometimes lighting a candle or wearing spider man or mermaid gear (to remind me of my children), but for you it could be anything that you do in memory of your loved one.

Choice Opportunity: Your Grief Ritual

Rituals are an important way for people to find meaning when they lose a loved one.
Rituals are a symbolic action to help express our feelings or keep an important part of the past alive.
Consider creating your own personal ritual.

What is the meaning of your ritual?	To connect with the loved one who has passed, carry on an activity they enjoyed, or celebrate a memory . . .	
When will the ritual happen?	You may want to do the ritual once a week, once a month or on special days.	
Where will the ritual take place?	You can choose a formal place like a church or cemetery or informal like a park or favorite restaurant.	
Who will be present?	The ritual can be done alone or with people.	
What activity will you choose to do?	Suggestions: a memorial service, light a candle a certain time of the day, visit the grave, spend time at a favorite spot, pray in their honor, write a letter, cook their favorite meal, make a donation in their honor . . .	

"This is what rituals are for. We do spiritual ceremonies as human beings in order to create a safe resting place for our most complicated feelings of joy or trauma, so that we don't have to haul those feelings around with us forever, weighing us down. We all need such places of ritual safekeeping. And I do believe that if your culture or tradition doesn't have the specific ritual you are craving, then you are absolutely permitted to make up a ceremony of your own devising, fixing your own broken-down emotional systems with all the do-it-yourself resourcefulness of a generous plumber/poet."

-- Elizabeth Gilbert, Eat, Pray, Love

This is your Choice Opportunity to be Mentally STRONG®

Day 6 – Dr. B's Experience

Theme: Going through the process.
Mood: Trying not to turn anger inward.

In the morning, as part of my meditation, I listened to a couple of sermons and then watched a series about grief. I cried during these activities but didn't find them overly valuable. One from William Worden provided a grief framework around four tasks: Accept Loss, Process, Adjust, and Find Connection. I just don't believe that the grieving process occurs in any order. It takes a conscious choice to have any order while processing intense grief and that's what I've been doing. And sometimes you continue to process what happened the previous day or days. That is what day six was about for me. I sat in the process mentally, spiritually, and emotionally. I thought about the events that happened the day before and the impact they had on my grief.

During my Controlled Grief in the afternoon, I got to a point of anger which was appropriate for me because I have been sitting in anger for some time. So, I tried to pinpoint the triggers of my anger. I am angered by what has happened to me and my family, and by people who talk like they've been there. Upon reflection, I concluded that I am most angry because I feel that what happened to me is not fair and that I don't deserve it.

When processing my anger, I often turn the pain inward and blame myself, or God, and then I get depressed. The anger mostly impacts my relationship with myself and not others. Generally, anger comes from a feeling of pain and injustice. Anger is easier to manage than grief though. This grief is what's hard. I would rather deal with my grief right now, but it's also important to unravel my anger as well.

There is not one thing that I can do to change my situation. I can wish it away as hard as possible, but nothing will alter it. It sucks a lot. It sucks pretty much more than anything has ever sucked. I often replace the word "sucks" with various curse words because there are no words to describe this pain. Time has not been my friend when it comes to grief. I am still waiting to heal, and I am still waiting for the ability to share my purpose.

Dr. B's Controlled Grief and 5 SELF's Process Day 6

Controlled Grief: I watched several series about grief that were recommended.

- **Spiritual Self**: I listened to a couple of sermons.
- **Self-Improvement:** I read Psychologist J. William Worden provides a framework of four tasks:
  - Accept loss
  - Process
  - Adjust
  - Find connection
- **Self-Movement:** I used a device that stimulates the brain called Alpha-Stim as movement.
- **Self-Regulation/Choose**: I watched a presentation on suicide that featured parents that were turning their pain into purpose. I was triggered by engaging in their story and pain but embraced it.
- **Self-Care:** I also considered the Alpha-Stim as my self-care for the day.

My Controlled Grief Journey Day 6   Date: /   /

What is your mood today?
(circle or fill in your own word)

Open	Loving	Sad	Guilty
Calm	Present	Depressed	Afraid
Relaxed	Safe	Broken Hearted	Overwhelmed
Hopeful	Angry	Irritable	Exhausted
Connected	Furious	Longing	Drained
Strong	Resentful	Disconnected	Numb

What activity did you choose to practice for **Controlled Grief**? _____

_____

What have you done today to empower your **Spiritual Self**? _____

_____

How did you practice **Self-Regulation** today? _____

_____

How were you able to work on **Self-Improvement** today? _____

_____

How were you able to prioritize your **Self-Care**? _____

_____

How were you able to work on **Self-Movement** today? _____

_____

Any other thoughts you want to remember about your **journey** today?

_____

Choice Opportunity of the day:
On Day 6, I realized how important it is to use the Mentally STRONG Method in grief. This Choice Opportunity includes a brief overview of the Mentally STRONG Method (the full method is in another book or course), to provide a glimpse into how to separate the things that you are dealing with so that you can make choices in line with your healing.

Choice Opportunity:

How to Use the Mentally STRONG Method in Grief

Objective: Learn how to use the Mentally STRONG Method as a grounding framework to identify, organize, process, cherish and grow in grief.

Step 1: Answer the following questions in the *Identify & Organize* Categories

Core Connections: Are there core negative beliefs about yourself that your loss intensities?	
Triggers: What are the environmental things, stimuli or comments people make that cause an intense emotional reaction?	
Grief:	
Trauma: What about your loss was traumatic?	
Negative Thoughts: What negative thoughts keep playing in your mind regarding yourself and your loss?	
Behaviors/Choices: What choices are you making that are impacting your healing?	
Anxiety/Worry: Since your loss, what do you worry about the most?	
Injustice: Is there a specific injustice/un-fairness associated with your loss?	
Spiritual Conflict: Are you angry, disheartened or hurt by an external belief system?	
Addiction: Have you developed addictive behaviors to cope with your loss?	

Learn more about *The Mentally STRONG Method*: 1-800-55-STRONG ~ www.mentallystrong.com

Step 2: Review the *GOALS* in the *Power of Choice* Categories and create your own Power of Choice to the right.

Core Connections: Improving your internal dialogue over time.	
Triggers: Develop insight and control over our external and internal responses and decreasing the impact of the trigger.	
Grief: Process and cherish.	
Trauma: Process and release.	
Negative Thoughts: Practice self-care and self-love as evidenced by speaking kindly to yourself.	
Behaviors/Choices: Make choices to care about and to love yourself.	
Anxiety/Worry: Decrease your anxiety to a level less than 5 (out of 10).	
Injustice: Keeping this category separate. Make choices on if and how you will counteract the injustice.	
Spiritual Conflict: Make a commitment to find your spiritual health.	
Addiction: Bring insight into the items above, treat any neurobiology and make choices that are healthy.	

This is your Choice Opportunity to be Mentally STRONG® in grief!

Learn more about *The Mentally STRONG Method*: 1-800-55-STRONG ~ www.mentallystrong.com

Day 7 - Dr. B's Experience

Theme: How much time do you need to grieve? Spiritual conflict.
Mood: Angry.

When I attempted to grieve in the morning, I realized that my anger was debilitating, and I didn't want to get out of bed. Every time I got up, I just wanted to get back under the covers. The anger didn't really subside until one or two o'clock. I meditated in the morning about my need to release my anger, anger related to the death of my children as well as other people and things that triggered me in the process.

I decided that my Controlled Grief that day would take place on the punching bag. I wrote down all the things that make me angry about what's happened and then taped them to the bag. I decided that later I would burn those words and hoped that I wouldn't catch anything on fire.

When I reflected upon my anger, I pinpointed the reasons. First, I'm angry because the whole experience has been spiritually confusing. I'm also angry because even when people want to help me, there's nothing they can do. It's my pain and I need to figure it out. I'm angry because I've had spiritual experiences with Miah and Reggie, but my Christian teaching makes it difficult to accept and trust it when it's happening. It's also been hard to connect with them on a regular basis which makes me angry too. I keep googling, looking for grief or spiritual retreats so that I can fill my cup, and hope that I can find someone who will help me. I'm mad because I can see why people get physically sick from grief. Sometimes I just don't want to get out of bed and that makes me angry. It would be so much easier to just tell people that I have a headache. But, if you don't take time to heal, you do get physically sick.

I'm also particularly angry because I spent 15 years trying to save my children. The whole time I tried to think positively while believing in myself, science, alternative medicine, and prayer, but I still lost my children. And, because of that, I've also lost my belief in myself. This process is so lonely, and I feel like I am looking for spiritual miracles. I don't like being alone. The only other person who's been through exactly what I've been through is my husband, and he's upstairs watching football. So, I am basically alone because he can't be present in the same way that I can. I'm angry that I have to go through this by myself.

I find that a lot of times, I don't know what to do with my anger. I mean, it helped a little bit to punch the punching bag and to burn those things written on paper that were making me angry. Still, it didn't get rid of my anger towards the fact that there was nothing I could do to save my kids no matter what I tried to do. Sometimes I feel like it is too much for one person. After Reggie died, I believed that God would never take both of my kids, but He did. I so badly want peace. I know that I have to feel the pain properly to process it, but I'm angry about how much it hurts. Sometimes I think it's worse for someone to actually be there, yet you are still alone (as I feel with Bundy). I'm angry that I cannot trust that when God speaks to me, He means it. He's spoken to me before and those things He promised did not come true. I'm angry because God is supposed to love me, and I don't feel like He does.

I sat with my anger for most of the morning, but eventually decided to go to yoga to see if I could move some of it out of my body. It's a gentle type of restorative yoga. My prayer and intention at yoga was to truly have a connection, and to trust that spiritual connection.

Upon reflection, I would say that one of the main things that came to me on this day was that there is an outer layer that's really preventing me from grieving- anger. I'm angry for so many reasons because it's confusing. People want to tell me that God is simple, but God is not simple. I want to feel peace in my heart, but I'm angry and it hurts. I'm even angry that there's no appropriate way to grieve and that it's easier to just say you're sick. Sometimes, it seems useless, but I know that I have to get it out of my body. It's been ten long years of praying and believing and I don't think that's enough.

I also spent a lot of time today trying to find somewhere I could go or someone that could help me heal spiritually. In the end, I decided that it's not a spiritual problem for me. I have to just keep going as it's my journey and only I can take it. I also concluded that the first step to grief or the first layer is releasing anger. Today, I engaged in that process by hitting the punching bag. I also continued with my own Self-Care and indulged in a chocolate covered apple. You can be sad but still take care of yourself, and so I did. The two are not mutually exclusive.

Dr. B's Controlled Grief and 5 SELF's Process Day 7

Controlled Grief: I punched the punching bag for anger.

- **Spiritual Self:** I focused on releasing anger.
- **Self-Improvement:** I studied biomarkers in grief and Kintsugi, a Japanese technique for preserving pottery, used as a healing from grief metaphor.
- **Self-Movement**: I participated in restorative yoga.
- **Self-Regulation/Choose**: Never giving up. I had all day to figure something out and I did.
- **Self-Care:** I enjoyed a chocolate covered apple.

My Controlled Grief Journey Day 7   Date: /   /

What is your mood today?
(circle or fill in your own word)

Open	Loving	Sad	Guilty
Calm	Present	Depressed	Afraid
Relaxed	Safe	Broken Hearted	Overwhelmed
Hopeful	Angry	Irritable	Exhausted
Connected	Furious	Longing	Drained
Strong	Resentful	Disconnected	Numb

What activity did you choose to practice for **Controlled Grief**? _____

_____

What have you done today to empower your **Spiritual Self**? _____

_____

How did you practice **Self-Regulation** today? _____

_____

How were you able to work on **Self-Improvement** today? _____

_____

How were you able to prioritize your **Self-Care**? _____

_____

How were you able to work on **Self-Movement** today? _____

_____

Any other thoughts you want to remember about your **journey** today?

_____

Choice Opportunity of the day:

On Day 7, I was hit hard with anger. I chose this Choice Opportunity, *Disable Your Forcefield*, because it's about disabling your protective layer. Sometimes people think that they don't get angry, but anger turned inward manifests as depression. So please complete this Choice Opportunity even if you don't believe you experience anger. Understanding and being conscious of whether you're protecting yourself will help in your healing.

Choice Opportunity: Disable the Forcefield of Anger

Significant loss or trauma can complicate your emotional equilibrium. The resulting pain can be unbearable.

Consequently, the profound event compels us to disengage from life and emit a protective force-field.

For many this forcefield takes on the emotion of anger which results in pushing people away or getting them to withdraw.

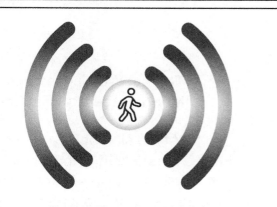

Describe the forcefield you have erected.	

Anger camouflages other emotions that are hiding beneath. Expressing anger can help disquise emotions that lay beneath the surface. Step back and become curious. What emotions are hiding beneath your anger?

❑ _____

❑ _____

❑ _____

❑ _____

❑ _____

Disabling the forcefield is the only option if we want to move forward with healing and peace. It is only possible if we set reasonable goals and work hard for them. Identify one emotion that was hidden beneath your anger and create small action steps to begin the disabling process.

What can I do now: Small steps immediately attainable today	

This is your Choice Opportunity to be *Mentally STRONG*®

Learn more about *The Mentally STRONG Method*: 1-800-55-STRONG ~ www.mentallystrong.com

* The Mentally STRONG Method with Choice Opportunities© Author: Cristi Bundukamara – not for reproduction/distribution

Day 8 - Dr. B's Experience

Theme: Working through grief and anger.
Mood: Understanding that there is also trauma.

At the start of Day 8, I was feeling good. I completed week one and believed that I had a strong start to the Controlled Grief process. But I felt like I was at the point where it was time to separate things. As you learned about with the Mentally STRONG method (see Appendix A for more information), we often let other things get enmeshed with our grief so it's important to sort that out.

I began my day with meditation followed by a Controlled Grief session. I went to the room that I decorated in honor of Miah and Reggie. The last time that I was in there, I took bags and bags of Miah's stuffed animals and threw them on the bed. I ended up laying on those stuffed treasures and just cried it out. There is so much pain still, and I'm working on my anger. As I sat there this time, I spotted a stuffed tiger and remembered a story from when Miah was little. I'd asked her what she thought Heaven would be like, and she paused for a moment and said, "I'd be allowed to play with the tigers."

Miah had never really understood why she couldn't play with tigers at the zoo. I'd forgotten about that because as she got older, she was really into mermaids. She loved all animals and had since told me that in heaven, she had a pet. It's a dog named Kojak. He's her best friend and as strong as a horse.

Smiling, I moved all of the stuffed tigers down to one spot. Miah would've liked that. I eyed a bear next to them that her boyfriend had given her for her birthday. There was another that I got her when I went out of town. It talks when you press it, saying "Mommy loves you." I also found a spiderman of Reggie's and tried to see if I could hang it from the ceiling. I decided to work on that later.

I was going to go through their clothes another day. It was too much for me at the moment. My breathing had become a bit irregular. A little at a time. I still didn't want to completely face the fact that my children were gone. Who would? Still, I was embracing the fact that they were, slowly, ever so slowly.

At the end of week one, going into week two, I concluded that it was not just grief that I was dealing with. It was also trauma and I need to start treating it as trauma.

Dr. B's Controlled Grief and 5 SELF's Process Day 8

Controlled Grief: I went through another box of stuffed toys.

- o **Spiritual Self:** On this day, my meditation and Controlled Grief were one and the same activity, as well as Yoga being both self-movement and spiritual self.
- o **Self-Improvement:** I studied *The 6 Rs of Mourning*.
- o **Self-Movement:** Yoga and embracing the opposite of anger which is gratitude.
- o **Self-Regulation/Choose**: I chose to acknowledge that I have trauma, not just grief.
- o **Self-Care**: I indulged in a 60-minute massage.

My Controlled Grief Journey Day 8

What is your mood today?
(circle or fill in your own word)

Open	Loving	Sad	Guilty
Calm	Present	Depressed	Afraid
Relaxed	Safe	Broken Hearted	Overwhelmed
Hopeful	Angry	Irritable	Exhausted
Connected	Furious	Longing	Drained
Strong	Resentful	Disconnected	Numb

What activity did you choose to practice for **Controlled Grief**? _____

_____

What have you done today to empower your **Spiritual Self**? _____

_____

How did you practice **Self-Regulation** today? _____

_____

How were you able to work on **Self-Improvement** today? _____

_____

How were you able to prioritize your **Self-Care**? _____

_____

How were you able to work on **Self-Movement** today? _____

_____

Any other thoughts you want to remember about your **journey** today?

_____

Choice Opportunity of the day:
On Day 8, I continued to work through my anger and grief, and selected this Choice Opportunity, *Getting Through Anger in Grief*, as an additional way to deal with my anger. It will help you to do the same.

Choice Opportunity: Getting Through Anger in Grief

Anger is an outer layer of protection. Anger helps us gain temporary control of our environment and helps us avoid the feelings of pain from grief. However, you will need to break through this layer of protection in order to allow healing to your broken heart.

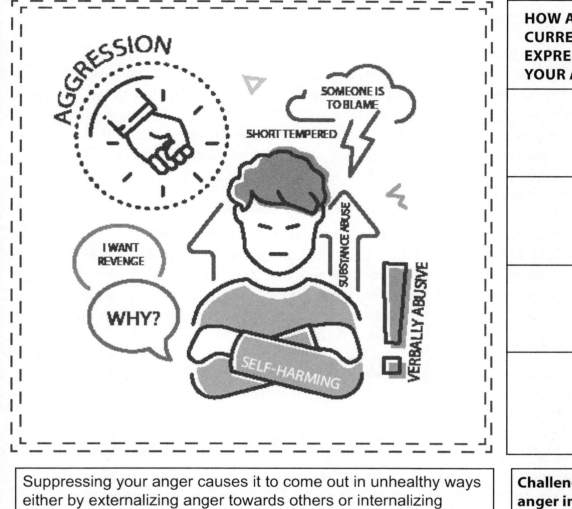

HOW ARE YOU CURRENTLY EXPRESSING YOUR ANGER?	RATE 0-10

Suppressing your anger causes it to come out in unhealthy ways either by externalizing anger towards others or internalizing towards yourself. Search online and choose a productive way you want to express your anger.

Rate your anger before you begin from 0-10. Ten being the highest. _____

_____
Technique I chose to release my anger.

Rate your anger when you finish from 0-10. Ten being the highest. _____

Challenge: Can you put your anger in a different category?

☐ core connection

☐ trauma

☐ negative thoughts

☐ behaviors/choices

☐ spiritual conflict

☐ injustice

This is your Choice Opportunity to be  Mentally STRONG®

Learn more about *The Mentally STRONG Method:* 1-800-55-STRONG ~ www.mentallystrong.com

*The Mentally STRONG Method with Choice Opportunities©Author: Cristi Bundukamara – not for reproduction/distribution

Day 9 – Dr. B's Experience

Theme: To connect and receive.
Mood: Busy but open and supported.

During my meditation in the morning, I set my intention for the Lakota Sweat Lodge scheduled for that night (an outing which involves a Native American spiritual experience and community). There were going to be a total of ten of us at the lodge: friends, family, and supporters of mine. My intention was to just be open to receive, to not try to control or move, but to take in what I could. Everyone on the journey with me had their own individual intentions. I'd participated in the Lakota Sweat Lodge before, a couple of months after Miah passed away. At that time, I just wanted to open that spiritual portal. Now, I wanted to dig deeper.

That morning, I also had an appointment with my doctor to get feedback regarding my SPECT scan. I was told that my brain shows a trauma response and that I need to address some of the physical signs of distress that the scan indicated. The problem is that I am more of a fixer for others. I really don't know how to take care of myself and receive care. That's one of the reasons that I decided that my intention for the Sweat Lodge was going to be the desire to receive.

Last week, I was kind of struggling with my expectations for myself related to being able to do all of the grief activities, and filming them for the documentary, and what people would say about it all. I always have the belief that I can do anything while figuring out how to do it on the fly. But that kind of thinking put me in fight or flight mode for the last 15 years. Because of that, a lot of history came out, and much of it was focused on my expectations of myself. And truthfully, now that I've seen the results of my scan, I would say that it definitely has affected my physical health. I'm probably just compensating really well because I have good coping skills. Some parts of my brain are on fire, about four or five times what they should be. And it just kind of hit me like a ton of bricks that I have been fighting for 15 years, probably since the day Johnny died.

I don't even know if I can work through the trauma right now because the first step in working through it is to distance yourself from the stress. But my husband has DRPLA, and I still have the responsibility to take care of him. I also have a lot of anticipatory fear related to him dying, and what will happen leading up to that point. At the same time, I must lean into identifying what my trauma is, and I'm not even sure that once I do, I can begin to process it.

Still, that's why using the Mentally STRONG Method is so effective. It helps people move through the pain. The identification of the trauma, and coming to understand it, is the catalyst for change. We can see where it originates which gives us a path to move forward. I spent the morning working through my trauma with one of our counselors. Although I am a practitioner, somebody that's worked in this industry for a long time, I am still not immune to the effects of trauma and its associated emotions. No one is.

Most of my thoughts during the day were related to the fresh news regarding the SPECT scan and some other busyness around the office and my home. I was still very excited about the Lakota Sweat Lodge and getting together with friends and family. The ceremony itself was very intense. We were sitting out in a circle in a teepee style tent which was pitch black. In the center were some heated stones which caused the tent to warm up quickly. The idea is to sweat out some of the things that you want to release. The water pourer led the ceremony, and everyone took turns stating their intentions to the universe. The water pourer next called out to the North, South, East and West and their associated animal spirits. Lastly, he called on the ancestors to hear everyone's intentions.

I embraced the spirit of receiving and laid down throughout the ceremony. I heard Miah say that she was trying to make everyone feel better. She also told me that Reggie thought we were all playing a game of duck, duck, goose which made me laugh. I felt like Reggie laid down on top of me, and that Miah was next to me. Those were their favorite positions to snuggle with me when they were alive.

Overall, it was a very positive experience for me. It helped unleash the stress of the day and allowed me to focus on my intention to receive. I was also happy to connect with both Miah and Reggie, and to be surrounded by family and friends during the grief journey. I felt less alone.

Journal

Use this page to journal any thoughts and feelings you may be experiencing along your journey:

_____

_____

_____

_____

_____

_____

_____

_____

_____

_____

_____

_____

_____

_____

_____

_____

_____

_____

_____

_____

_____

_____

Dr. B's Controlled Grief and 5 SELF's Process Day 9

Controlled Grief Activity: Energetic experience with Miah and Reggie in the Lakota Sweat lodge.

- o **Spiritual Self:** Lakota Sweat Lodge is the perfect meditation environment.
- o **Self-Improvement**: I went to the Lakota Sweat Lodge. With preparation, the actual activity, and social process.
- o **Self-Movement**: Lakota Sweat Lodge, the physical act of sweating as my movement.
- o **Self-Regulation/Choose**: Lakota Sweat Lodge as a well-rounded strategy.
- o **Self-Care:** Lakota Sweat Lodge. On this day, the act of preparation, social process and the actual ceremony were all the elements of my daily grieving.

My Controlled Grief Journey Day 9

Date: / /

What is your mood today?
(circle or fill in your own word)

Open	Loving	Sad	Guilty
Calm	Present	Depressed	Afraid
Relaxed	Safe	Broken Hearted	Overwhelmed
Hopeful	Angry	Irritable	Exhausted
Connected	Furious	Longing	Drained
Strong	Resentful	Disconnected	Numb

What activity did you choose to practice for **Controlled Grief**? _____

_____

What have you done today to empower your **Spiritual Self**? _____

_____

How did you practice **Self-Regulation** today? _____

_____

How were you able to work on **Self-Improvement** today? _____

_____

How were you able to prioritize your **Self-Care**? _____

_____

How were you able to work on **Self-Movement** today? _____

_____

Any other thoughts you want to remember about your **journey** today?

_____

Choice Opportunity of the day:
While moving through this process, it hit me that many of us have also experienced trauma as part of our grief and/or have gone through other types of traumas in our lives that have intensified during our grief. This Choice Opportunity is like the one that you've completed about grief but different because it addresses trauma.

Choice Opportunity:

How to Use the Mentally STRONG Method in Trauma

Objective: Learn how to use the Mentally STRONG Method as a grounding framework to safely identify and unpack, organize, process, and grow post trauma.

Step 1: Psychoeducation Use the Identify and Organize worksheet to complete the 10 categories using the questions below.

Core Connections: You likely have core beliefs that originated during trauma, list those in this category.	
Triggers: What external stimuli triggers you to remember or experience an emotional trauma?	
Grief: What have you lost as a result of your trauma?	
Trauma: Complete the Choice Opportunity: "Impact of Trauma"	
Negative Thoughts: What negative thoughts do you have about yourself that are associated with your trauma?	
Behaviors/Choices: Have you made unhealthy choices as a maladaptive coping strategy?	
Anxiety/Worry: What do you worry about related to the trauma you have experienced?	
Injustice: Identify the injustice in the trauma you experienced.	
Spiritual Conflict: If there is a divine source that is loving and protective, what doesn't make sense about the trauma you experienced?	
Addiction: Do you engage in addictive behavior as a maladaptive coping from your trauma?	

Learn more about *The Mentally STRONG Method*: 1-800-55-STRONG ~ www.mentallystrong.com

Step 2: Desensitization and Integration

How to process trauma:

> *Step 1:* Bring the traumatic event into consciousness, focus on the event.
>
> *Step 2:* Feel the emotions that come up
>
> *Step 3:* Engage in physical movement until the intensity decreases
>
> *Step 4:* Self Regulate, tap into your healthy coping skills learned from psychoeducation
>
> *Step 5:* Repeat as needed

Additional resources for processing:

Professional	Personal
Cognitive Behavioral	Conscious movement
Ketamine Assisted	Prayer or Meditation
Narrative Exposure	Spiritual Rituals
Brainspotting	Yoga
EMDR	Various Energy Practices
MeRT – TMS	EFT (Emotional Freedom Technique)
Imaginal Exposure	Music or Vibration
Accelerated Resolution	Dancing
Hypnotherapy	

Step 3: Posttraumatic Growth

Continue the process of steps 2 and 3 until the impact of the traumatic event is at a manageable level. Refer to the Impact of Trauma Choice Opportunity worksheet.

This is your Choice Opportunity to be Mentally STRONG® in posttraumatic growth!

Learn more about *The Mentally STRONG Method*: 1-800-55-STRONG ~ www.mentallystrong.com

Day 10 - Dr. B's Experience

Theme: Grief with gratitude.
Mood: Trying to breathe and understand.

I began the day by going into Controlled Grief, entering Miah and Reggie's room. I was smiling but knew that it wouldn't last for very long. Looking around, I thought that I had put away all of the stuffed animals but saw that there were still some more of Miah's lying here and there. I also noticed a coloring book of cards and thought that I probably should take some time to color. There were so many Barbies too! Miah had all of them and every mermaid possible. Next, I spotted another coloring book that I'd bought for Miah. It said, "I'm strong." It's funny how that was the only one that she'd decided to color. But then I noticed another one that said, "I am beautiful." It was shaded with purple and pink. That she was. Strong and beautiful. When I bought them, I thought that maybe these books would help her with her reading. That was when I was more optimistic about the disease.

I used to try to get Miah to organize her purses and there they still were. I figured that I would probably keep them. I found a red one that I bought her when I went to Italy. I also found a little stuffed animal of Reggie's that Miah kept reminding her of him. It was nice but looking at it in that moment made me start to cry. The reality of it was just so sad. I didn't understand. It hurts so much, and going through these boxes is like rubbing salt in the wounds.

I looked around and spotted her sparkly headbands and the goggles that she used when she went swimming. She had like 10 or 20 pairs. It is so hard to make decisions about what to keep and what to give away. It is like giving away pieces of them, no matter how small they seem. And I still have at least another ten boxes to go through. This was just the beginning.

Yet, I want kids to be able to play with their stuff and I will keep some for my grandchildren. During that moment, I was torn between wanting to laugh and wanting to just throw something. I did feel like I released some of my anger and leaned into my grief during the process despite my bubbling feelings of despair.

I didn't get to my meditation until like 9 PM or something that evening. The day before, I had my meditation in the Lakota Sweat Lodge. The day before that, it was in yoga class. I wrote on post-it's at the front of my mat about things that were the opposite of anger. They were around gratefulness and there are tons of things that I'm grateful for. Still, stating those things doesn't decrease the pain I'm going through.

"Think.

Organize.

Choose."

~ Dr. B

Use this page to journal any thoughts and feelings you may be experiencing along your journey:

_____

_____

_____

_____

_____

_____

_____

_____

_____

_____

_____

_____

_____

_____

_____

_____

_____

_____

_____

_____

_____

_____

_____

I reflected upon something else that had happened during the day. I'd watched one of the nurse practitioners at my Mentally STRONG clinic take a patient who was very worked up and just had him breathe. In yoga and other spiritual practices, we say that breath is life. After breathing for three or four seconds, I know that there is a whole world, the universe, and God. I am able to connect with all that's outside of my little brain, much of which I don't understand. I don't even know if we're capable of understanding. I was breathing, but I felt tired. I was tired of everything being so difficult and losing. I fought so hard for my children. I tried to lean into gratefulness. I focused on the fact that I am so grateful that I got to be their mother, that they taught me how to fight (Reggie) and showed me what it was like to be content (Miah). I don't have to fight anymore, but I still don't know how to be content.

After some time, it came to me. There are layers of grief, not steps. There's this outer layer of protection and sometimes that's taken over by anger or else we mask what's there by putting on a pretty face. Sometimes, that layer involves avoiding things and trying to protect our heart because it is so painful. As Reggie said to me, "One day, you'll understand." And during this meditation, I wanted to believe that.

Dr. B's Controlled Grief and 5 SELF's Process Day 10

Controlled Grief: I went through three more boxes of Miah's belongings.

- o **Spiritual Self:** I watched the video: *Dear God and Gratitude*.
- o **Self-Improvement:** I didn't study anything specific this day but continue to be committed to my self-improvement.
- o **Self-Movement:** I walked on the treadmill while creating the reconnection after grief.
- o **Self-Regulation:** Although I didn't identify anything specific this day, I always have to use my self-regulation skills to function especially when actively grieving.
- o **Self-Care:** Nothing specific on this day.

My Controlled Grief Journey Day 10

Date: / /

What is your mood today?
(circle or fill in your own word)

Open	Loving	Sad	Guilty
Calm	Present	Depressed	Afraid
Relaxed	Safe	Broken Hearted	Overwhelmed
Hopeful	Angry	Irritable	Exhausted
Connected	Furious	Longing	Drained
Strong	Resentful	Disconnected	Numb

What activity did you choose to practice for **Controlled Grief**? _____

_____

What have you done today to empower your **Spiritual Self**? _____

_____

How did you practice **Self-Regulation** today? _____

_____

How were you able to work on **Self-Improvement** today? _____

_____

How were you able to prioritize your **Self-Care**? _____

_____

How were you able to work on **Self-Movement** today? _____

_____

Any other thoughts you want to remember about your **journey** today?

_____

Choice Opportunity of the day:
On Day 10, I challenge you to combat your anger. *Gratefulness is the opposite of anger.*
So, when you find yourself getting angry, search for those things that you are grateful
for (they are still there despite your loss).

Choice Opportunity: Grateful is the Opposite of Anger

If you are triggered by the statement "Be Grateful" I challenge you to complete this Choice Opportunity. Often when I hear "Gratefulness is the key to happiness" or similar statements it triggers anger. Take some time to process through the "why".

What do you have a RIGHT to be angry about?

How is that anger impacting you physically, mentally, or spiritually?

Do an internet search of insightful anger quotes. Write down the top three that resonate with you.

Considering these things - what are you grateful for?

This is your Choice Opportunity to be Mentally STRONG®

Learn more about *The Mentally STRONG Method*: 1-800-55-STRONG ~ www.mentallystrong.com

*The Mentally STRONG Method with Choice Opportunities© Author: Cristi Bundukamara – not for reproduction/distribution

Day 11 – Dr. B's Experience

Theme: Rest and Self-Care.
Mood: Reflective.

On Day 11, I was physically, mentally, and emotionally exhausted. I had a head cold and rested all day. Because of that, I didn't set aside any official time for meditation, but I was really thinking deeply about grief and my journey all day. I meditated on trying to avoid having a fight or flight response to things around me. I also updated my journal and caught up on some things related to the 45 Day Grief journey. Additionally, I took some time to dig deeper into my SPECT scan results and thought a lot about the trauma that they indicated as well as the possibility that something could be wrong with me physically. I was worried and called my father to discuss the results and the fact that I have been living with trauma for such an extensive period of time. We also talked a lot about Reggie and Miah. Crying together was a good release for me.

Later, I spent some time in the jacuzzi and thought about the best way for me to honor my loved ones. I landed on the fact that I could go to South Florida and revisit some of the places that are special to my family. Dolphin therapy was one of Reggie and Miah's favorite activities so I called to see if we could get an appointment there and set it up for the week after Thanksgiving. My sister and I decided that we would fly down and do a "weeping walk" around South Florida, visiting the places where memories of Reggie and Miah are the strongest.

Overall, it was a mixed day. There were moments of hope and moments of despair. My big takeaway, however, was when I concluded that I needed to learn how to rest and take some serious time to heal from the trauma. I feel like I have been in a burning house for the last 15 years, trying to pull my kids out, but having to watch them burn to death instead. Stressful doesn't even begin to describe it.

Dr. B's Controlled Grief and 5 SELF's Process Day 11

Controlled Grief: I called my dad and talked about Reggie and Miah and all the trauma that I have experienced over the past 15 years. I cried with my dad, acknowledging that I have been in a trauma response for a long time.

- **Spiritual Self**: No official time of prayer and meditation, but I had a lot of introspection throughout the day.
- **Self-Improvement**: None today.
- **Self-Movement:** I spent some time in the jacuzzi.
- **Self-Regulation/Choose:** I talked myself down when The Harvard Brain Bank said that they found something when testing Miah's brain. I rationalized that I don't need to respond in fight or flight.
- **Self-Care:** I rested, which is very hard for me, and even canceled an obligation. I realized that I am too emotionally stressed to continue at this pace.

My Controlled Grief Journey Day 11   Date: /   /

What is your mood today?
(circle or fill in your own word)

Open	Loving	Sad	Guilty
Calm	Present	Depressed	Afraid
Relaxed	Safe	Broken Hearted	Overwhelmed
Hopeful	Angry	Irritable	Exhausted
Connected	Furious	Longing	Drained
Strong	Resentful	Disconnected	Numb

What activity did you choose to practice for **Controlled Grief**? _____

_____

What have you done today to empower your **Spiritual Self**? _____

_____

How did you practice **Self-Regulation** today? _____

_____

How were you able to work on **Self-Improvement** today? _____

_____

How were you able to prioritize your **Self-Care**? _____

_____

How were you able to work on **Self-Movement** today? _____

_____

Any other thoughts you want to remember about your **journey** today?

_____

Choice Opportunity of the Day:

For Day 11, I chose *Mapping Cumulative Grief*. Even if you had only one intense loss, there could be some cumulative grief around that. For example, you might have lost your son but then lost some other relationships after that (as a result of the initial loss). Maybe you experienced a related financial loss, or some other type of loss in conjunction. This Choice Opportunity allows you to map out what else you have lost.

Choice Opportunity: Mapping Cumulative Grief

The objective of this choice opportunity is for you to identify what you have learned about grief over the years. List your different losses and then reflect on how you processed the grief. How did you react? How did you respond to others? How did others interact with you? What were your emotions and thoughts about the loss?

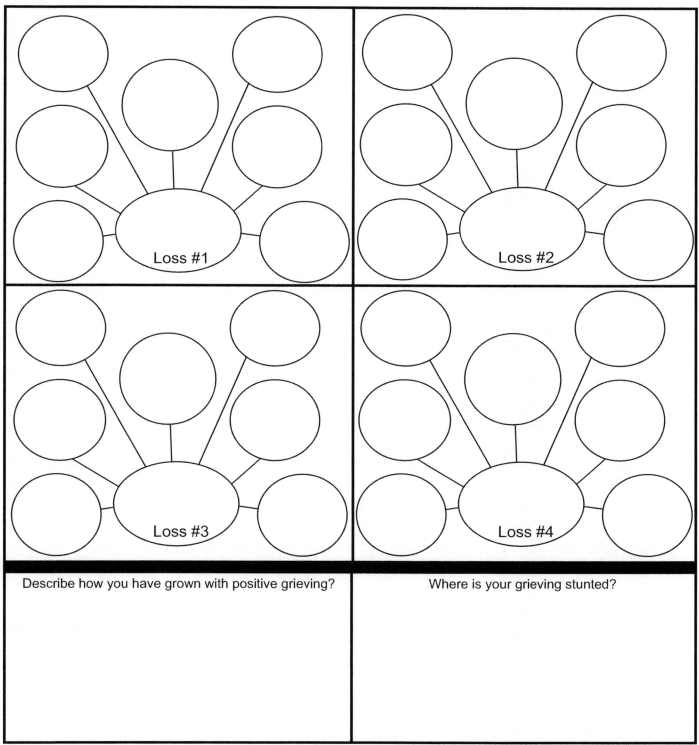

Loss #1

Loss #2

Loss #3

Loss #4

Describe how you have grown with positive grieving?

Where is your grieving stunted?

This is your Choice Opportunity to be Mentally STRONG®

Learn more about *The Mentally STRONG Method*: 1-800-55-STRONG ~ www.mentallystrong.com

Day 12 - Dr. B's Experience

Theme: Connection and letting go.
Mood: Connecting to your loved one. All that I have experienced was confirmed.

Going into another morning of Controlled Grief, I grabbed a few more boxes of Miah's things and tried to organize them. I decided that I wanted to start by doing an exercise from another workbook. I was creating this book at the time but wanted to experience everything else that's out there too. There are years of research that people have already done about grief. I fumbled through this new workbook and realized that it had different worksheets, like mine. I found one worksheet that was appropriate. It had a question: What will you do? So, I concluded that instead it should be (in the current moment): What should I do with my memories? I felt that there were memories to keep and savor, and others to put aside and return to later.

On my journey the day before, I had an epiphany regarding the need to separate my grief and trauma because grief needs to be cherished and trauma should be released. What do I do with my memories right now in these 45 days of grief? I want to keep and savor memories about how happy both Reggie and Miah were despite everything. The memories that I'm going to put aside (to deal with as trauma later) are those related to their DRPLA and suffering.

My children loved colorful things. They gave me purpose when they were alive and an understanding of a spiritual realm after they passed. As I go through these items, each time I look at a toy, I often get a memory of when I bought it or how they got it. Then, at other times, I just look at it as a bunch of junk. But I go through all of it still as part of my Controlled Grief process. When we take the time to really think about our loved ones, we make decisions based on their personalities. For example, we put Reggie's ashes in a circle because ever since he could crawl, he would run circles around people. And Miah was given the lotus flower because she really was the sweetest, purest soul that I have ever met and will ever know.

I decided to tackle the bin of mermaids and tiaras that Miah so dearly loved. She, without a doubt, wanted to be a princess and a mermaid. There were also a lot of spider man toys, Reggie's favorite superhero. Finding a spot for all of it including some costume jewelry, I thought more about how it didn't make sense that they had to die.

I also recalled why we moved to Colorado in the first place. People were flocking here because this little girl named Charlotte was able to control her seizures using a substance called Charlotte's Web. There was so much hope, but still Reggie died. And then Charlotte actually died, followed by other kids in our community. Each blow was heart wrenching. And then it was Miah. It's so hard to believe in a loving God when children are dying. I realized that I was bringing my spiritual conflict into my grief. It was not about God, though, and I'd figure that piece out later.

So many toys. I didn't even like toys. I never played with Miah, that was not my style. I feel guilty about that and wish that I had played more, but I was not that type of Mom. I was too busy fighting and trying to make sure everything was okay. There's that fight again. Because there is no going back, I reminded myself that I did the best I could to be a good Mom and to manage everything. My children were my true loves after all, even though I didn't always show it perfectly. It was always in my heart.

Later that day, Bundy and I met with a medium, Troy. Bundy has had a hard time connecting with Reggie and Miah since they passed. I was skeptical about using a medium but wanted to be open to all methods of connecting. Troy said that he was there to tell us what came through and then answer our questions. He was a born again Christian and said that his information comes from God or Jesus. Our medium considered himself a sort of bereavement counselor but told me that we all have the ability to connect. Our intuition gets stronger as we get older too.

Troy was able to connect with Miah first who told us that she had two younger brothers with her, even though in reality, they were her older brothers. Because she passed away at an older age than they did, she claimed that they were younger. Miah reassured us that they are all right, and that they were together. She also talked about watching out for Bundy. Miah said that before Bundy passed, he would see her and know that it was time. Bundy's mother also came through and told us that we shouldn't worry, that she was watching over everyone and had it under control. It was good to get those reassurances.

We also got to hear from Johnny too, which was wonderful. Bundy and I had less time with him than our other children. Johnny reassured us that he loved us and considered us his parents. He was happy that we helped him discover God and Jesus before he passed. Johnny was always quiet but said that it was only because he'd experienced so much trauma in his life. He felt that the time he spent with us was the calmest though and told us that we'd played an important role in his life. The message was very validating.

At the end of the session, we were allowed to ask questions. The main question that I had involved whether Miah had a choice when it came to dying. Miah said that she didn't want to hurt our feelings but that she did have a choice. She didn't want to be a

"Regardless of your story, you can choose strength. And eventually, joy."
~ Dr. B

Use this page to journal any thoughts and feelings you may be experiencing along your journey:

_____

_____

_____

_____

_____

_____

_____

_____

_____

_____

_____

_____

_____

_____

_____

_____

_____

_____

_____

_____

_____

_____

burden and didn't want us taking care of her. Miah told us that she wanted us to be free to take care of others, and somehow that made me feel better. She felt us there with her the whole time. Troy confirmed that she is now a guardian angel and I believe that is the perfect role for her. It was a powerful experience and gave us both a lot of peace.

Dr. B's Controlled Grief and 5 SELF's Process Day 12

Controlled Grief: I went through more boxes of toys.

- o **Spiritual Self:** I spoke with a Medium (Troy). Bundy and I connected with Reggie, Johnny, and Miah.
- o **Self-Improvement:** I started reading the book *The Grieving Brain.*
- o **Self-Movement:** No specific movement today.
- o **Self-Regulation/Choose:** I made a choice to receive and trust my intuition.
- o **Self-Care:** I engaged in HBOT (Hyperbaric Oxygen Therapy).

My Controlled Grief Journey Day 12

Date: /   /

What is your mood today?
(circle or fill in your own word)

Open	Loving	Sad	Guilty
Calm	Present	Depressed	Afraid
Relaxed	Safe	Broken Hearted	Overwhelmed
Hopeful	Angry	Irritable	Exhausted
Connected	Furious	Longing	Drained
Strong	Resentful	Disconnected	Numb

What activity did you choose to practice for **Controlled Grief**? _____

_____

What have you done today to empower your **Spiritual Self**? _____

_____

How did you practice **Self-Regulation** today? _____

_____

How were you able to work on **Self-Improvement** today? _____

_____

How were you able to prioritize your **Self-Care**? _____

_____

How were you able to work on **Self-Movement** today? _____

_____

Any other thoughts you want to remember about your **journey** today?

_____

Choice Opportunity of the day:

For Day 12, I chose *The Emotional Teapot* Choice Opportunity. If we don't work through our grief and emotions, it's like a teapot with the lid sealed shut. You will eventually explode! So, letting the intensity out every once in a while, is an important part of the healing process.

Choice Opportunity: Emotional Teapot Theory

Expected outcome: Understand the results of stuffing or not processing your emotions or feelings. Learn how to understand the emotions and feelings better. **THIS IS NOT FOR ANXIETY:** Ruminating on your worry can worsen your anxiety.

A boiling teapot is a good way to see the effects of your feelings within you when you refuse to recognize, process, or feel those feelings from your life experiences.

Your feelings, like the boiling water, need to escape from the vessel periodically. This is a relief valve in the design of the teapot. What happens if you block that release valve in the teapot?_____

You are no different than the teapot. You need a release of the feelings. You cannot stuff or bottle up those feelings over an extended period of time in a healthy manner.

The practice of refusing to acknowledge, feel, or process the feelings will change you. This will have an impact on who you are. This will have a negative impact on you as a person in many areas: emotional, mental, physical health, and within your social life. It is important to recognize the behaviors of stuffing your feelings. You are choosing to avoid your feelings. You are choosing to avoid feeling. Now is the time to recognize and change that practice.

What feelings are your refusing to feel with stuffing, blocking, or ignoring the feelings?

_____

_____

_____

_____

Learn more about *The Mentally STRONG Method*: 1-800-55-STRONG ~ www.mentallystrong.com

What do you think will happen if you continue to refuse to feel these feelings?

_____

_____

_____

_____

What could happen if you start acknowledging and feeling these feelings?

Mental	Emotional	Physical	Spiritual

How will you release the pressure in your teapot and begin to let off steam? How will you feel those feelings or express yourself in healthy ways to improve your mental health?

_____

_____

_____

What choices will you make to let go in a safe way to experience the feelings and to be heard?

_____

_____

_____

Day 13 – Dr. B's Experience

Theme: Processing new information.
Mood: Introspective.

During my morning meditation, I processed the information that Bundy and I received from the medium. I kept coming back to the fact that Miah had a choice and leaving us was her choice. That made me feel better about the way that it happened. There wasn't something that I missed. A choice is much different than an error or omission. I focused on trying to connect with Miah and talking to her about her decision to leave us. I wanted her to know that I supported her no matter what in all of her decisions and that I loved her.

Later, I reflected even further on the messages. I felt more peaceful, like perhaps there was a purpose to it all. Part of my job would also be to help get Bundy ready to pass. It made me feel better that Miah, Reggie, Johnny, and many others would be waiting for him on the other side and that he was already so strong spiritually.

I listened to more from *The Grieving Brain* by Mary Francis O'Conner and continued to find it quite interesting, not only in relation to my own situation but for the others that I treat as well. I hope to dive even further into the subject of grief and its impact on the brain. She talked about seeing a specialist in complicated grief therapy, which I thought would be really good for people who feel like they need professional help. I could potentially interview one, but I don't feel like I need to go through my whole process with them. I'm going through that right now with my method. It's a cognitive behavioral model and is already working through all of those pieces.

In the evening, as a form of self-care, I decided to go to a comedy club with my sister. At first, I thought that I didn't want to go because I was feeling down. In the end, I chose to go and lift myself up, but it would have been okay if I chose to stay home too. Self-regulation is a personal choice. In the end, I was happy with my decision. It was great to be able to get out there and laugh for a while. The comedians were so funny, and I really needed a mental distraction from processing all of the information, grief, and trauma that I've been diving into. I was so grateful for my sister, not just that night, but always. She has been such a tremendous support system throughout all that has been happening around me, and to me.

Journal

Use this page to journal any thoughts and feelings you may be experiencing along your journey:

_____

_____

_____

_____

_____

_____

_____

_____

_____

_____

_____

_____

_____

_____

_____

_____

_____

_____

_____

_____

_____

_____

_____

Dr. B's Controlled Grief and 5 SELF's Process Day 13

Controlled Grief: Many hours of reflecting on my grief.

- o **Spiritual Self:** Processing the mediumship. I talked with Miah today about her choice.
- o **Self-Improvement:** I continued reading the book *The Grieving Brain*. I emailed and requested an interview with the author.
- o **Self-Movement:** Jacuzzi alone while reflecting.
- o **Self-Regulation/Choose:** Making the choice to go out with my sister actually took some self-regulation. I was feeling down and could have chosen to stay down if I wanted to (but decided not to).
- o **Self-Care:** Hyperbaric oxygen therapy and laughing with my sister.

My Controlled Grief Journey Day 13

Date: / /

What is your mood today?
(circle or fill in your own word)

Open	Loving	Sad	Guilty
Calm	Present	Depressed	Afraid
Relaxed	Safe	Broken Hearted	Overwhelmed
Hopeful	Angry	Irritable	Exhausted
Connected	Furious	Longing	Drained
Strong	Resentful	Disconnected	Numb

What activity did you choose to practice for **Controlled Grief**? _____

_____

What have you done today to empower your **Spiritual Self**? _____

_____

How did you practice **Self-Regulation** today? _____

_____

How were you able to work on **Self-Improvement** today? _____

_____

How were you able to prioritize your **Self-Care**? _____

_____

How were you able to work on **Self-Movement** today? _____

_____

Any other thoughts you want to remember about your **journey** today?

_____

Choice Opportunity of the day:

On Day 13, I chose the Choice Opportunity *Process Differently* which I created during my 45 days of grief. I realized that my husband and I (as well as others who loved my children) were processing grief differently. Despite those differences, there were still ways to come together in grief.

Choice Opportunity: Process Differently

It is sometimes difficult to heal after experiencing a loss because of the overwhelming and overlapping emotions. Often times a loss is associated with a sudden and unexpected traumatic experience. Take time to acknowledge the layers of emotions. Grief and trauma are processed differently in our mental, spiritual, physical, and emotional being.

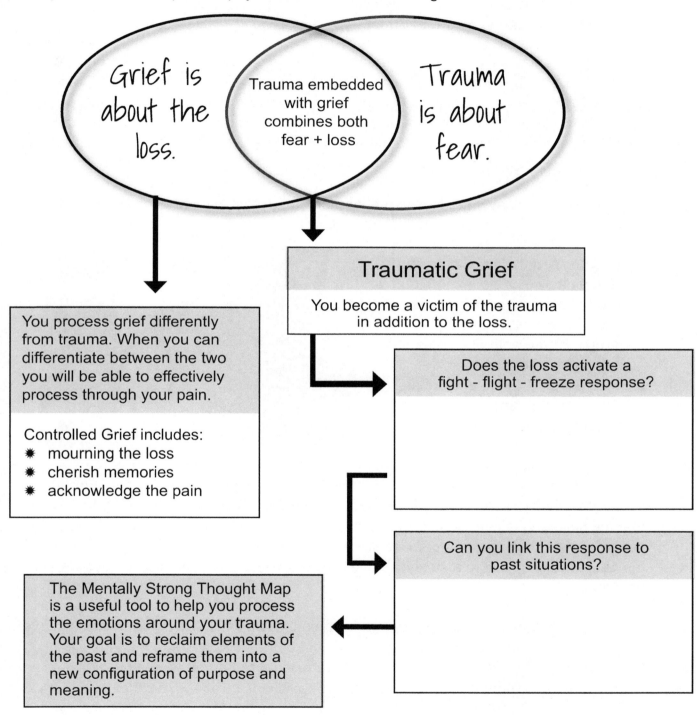

Grief is about the loss.

Trauma embedded with grief combines both fear + loss

Trauma is about fear.

You process grief differently from trauma. When you can differentiate between the two you will be able to effectively process through your pain.

Controlled Grief includes:
* mourning the loss
* cherish memories
* acknowledge the pain

Traumatic Grief

You become a victim of the trauma in addition to the loss.

Does the loss activate a fight - flight - freeze response?

Can you link this response to past situations?

The Mentally Strong Thought Map is a useful tool to help you process the emotions around your trauma. Your goal is to reclaim elements of the past and reframe them into a new configuration of purpose and meaning.

This is your Choice Opportunity to be Mentally STRONG®

Learn more about *The Mentally STRONG Method*: 1-800-55-STRONG ~ www.mentallystrong.com

*The Mentally STRONG Method with Choice Opportunities© Author: Cristi Bundukamara – not for reproduction/distribution

Day 14 – Dr. B's Experience

Theme: Understanding and appreciation.
Mood: Happy to spend time with Bundy.

Day 14 was a bit of a breakthrough day for me. I was finishing my second week of grief and growing more confident every day that I was doing the right thing. During my evening meditation, God revealed that it was better for Him to take Bundy than having him stay and suffer. As I mentioned, I've been going through a lot of spiritual conflict. I have been struggling with the fact that God would take three of my children and that my husband would suffer in the way that he has. But today, I felt a lot of resolution in my relationship with God, like I had a greater understanding of his master plan for it all, and that He still loved me. I made an active choice to remember this feeling when I am wrestling with God in the future.

I decided that my Controlled Grief that day would be going through pictures of our children with Bundy. The photos brought back so many memories for the both of us, and I was glad that I included Bundy in the process. Reggie, Miah, and Johnny were our children after all. There is no one else who could share in this grief as much as him.

Bundy was sad going through the memories, as was I. We had pictures from vacations and everyday activities. We recalled our trip to Hawaii and many of the things that the children loved to do. It turned out that I really needed this focused time with my husband after dealing with the anticipatory grief related to him, and in many respects, the deterioration of our relationship. I love my husband, but it's hard not to miss what we once had.

My movement on this day was walking on the treadmill. It is so important to move when we are grieving, and to try to get things out of the body. We should drink plenty of water too, which I don't always do. I have to remind myself more about that. While walking, I had an Alpha-Stim on which was doing little stimulations to either side of my ear. The point of the Alpha-Stim is to help organize my brain. It is something that can help with both my anxiety and trauma. I've always been a bit of a multitasker so I'm walking (moving the grief), using the Alpha-Stim (Self-Care), and reflecting on my grief (more introspection). I was also thinking about Dual Theory, a grief theory that I was learning about. It's actually one of the most well-respected grief theories right now.

Dual Theory talks about an oscillation where you're going back and forth between your brain and your emotions, mentally and physically switching between them. A grieving person is impacted by stressors that come from focusing on and processing the loss of a person who died. This includes everything that you do like looking at old photos which is restoration orientation, to loss orientation (focusing on the loss), and back to restoration orientation. Looking through pictures is what I describe as Controlled Grief. You get to choose when you do that rather than being triggered from the outside. Restoration orientation is where you're thinking about grief for the person that has died, including feelings of isolation, and the rebuilding that must happen in everyday life. Going back and forth involves the concept of oscillating. It means engaging in a dynamic process of switching between loss and restoration, just what I talk about with Controlled Grief, and it makes perfect sense. The griever will oscillate between confronting the loss and avoiding the loss.

But what I've noticed is that when you have intense grief or trauma, other things in your life get enmeshed with that grief. And so, although these theories are great, and this one seems to be very good, you have to incorporate Controlled Grief into your process as well. I always say that if you don't take the time for Controlled Grief, it will come up intrusively when you don't want it to. I encourage you to take the allotted time for your loss orientation and do your Controlled Grief so that you can spend some time in restoration. That's exactly what I am doing during these 45 days.

Dr. B's Controlled Grief and 5 SELF's Process Day 14

Controlled Grief: I went through pictures with Bundy.

- o **Spiritual Self:** I had a moment of peace feeling the eternal presence of my family.
- o **Self-Improvement:** I researched Dual Process Theory.
- o **Self-Movement:** I walked on the treadmill.
- o **Self-Regulation/Choose:** Spiritual conflict. I feel lots of resolution in my relationship with God today. I chose to remember this feeling when I am wrestling with God in the future.
- o **Self-Care:** I allowed someone else to pay and take Bundy and I to the movies with the grandkids.

My Controlled Grief Journey Day 14

Date: /   /

What is your mood today?
(circle or fill in your own word)

Open	Loving	Sad	Guilty
Calm	Present	Depressed	Afraid
Relaxed	Safe	Broken Hearted	Overwhelmed
Hopeful	Angry	Irritable	Exhausted
Connected	Furious	Longing	Drained
Strong	Resentful	Disconnected	Numb

What activity did you choose to practice for **Controlled Grief**? _____

_____

What have you done today to empower your **Spiritual Self**? _____

_____

How did you practice **Self-Regulation** today? _____

_____

How were you able to work on **Self-Improvement** today? _____

_____

How were you able to prioritize your **Self-Care**? _____

_____

How were you able to work on **Self-Movement** today? _____

_____

Any other thoughts you want to remember about your **journey** today?

_____

Choice Opportunity of the day:

For Day 14, I chose the *Healing and Derailers in Grief* Choice Opportunity. It was derived from an acronym that resonated with me. This exercise helps you to focus on healing as well as the derailing things that happen to all of us. What choices can you make to move away from the derailers?

Choice Opportunity: Healing and Derailers in Grief

HEALING Milestones

H Honor your loved one and yourself; discover your own interests and values.

E Ease emotional pain; open yourself to emotions, both painful and pleasant ones; trust that you can deal with emotional pain; it doesn't control you.

A Accept grief and let it find a place in your life.

L Learn to live with reminders of your loss.

I Integrate memories of your loved one; let them enrich your life, and help you learn and grow.

N Narrate stories of the death for yourself; share them with others.

G Gather others around you; connect with your community, let people in and let them suppport you.

DERAILERS

D Doubt that you did enough for the person who died.

E Embracing ideas about grief that make you want to change it or control it.

R Repeatedly imagining scenarios where the death didn't happen or happened differently, "if only" thinking.

A Anger and bitterness you can't resolve or let go of.

I Insistent belief this death was unfair or wrong or shouldn't have happened.

L Lack of faith in the possibility of adapting to the loss and having a promising future.

E Excessive avoidance of reminders of the loss.

R Rejecting support from others, unable to let others help, feeling hurt and alone.

S Survivor guilt is stopping you from experiencing joy and satisfaction.

Source: M. Katherine Shear, MD. Center for Complicated Grief, Columbia University

Describe how you have been moving in and out and through the HEALING milestones.

Consider where you have been derailed. How can you resolve them and set them aside?

This is your Choice Opportunity to be  Mentally STRONG®

Learn more about *The Mentally STRONG Method:* 1-800-55-STRONG ~ www.mentallystrong.com

Day 15 – Dr. B's Experience

Theme: Patience with the process.
Mood: Panic followed by calm.

As I started Day 15, during my morning meditation, I realized that it's been such a rollercoaster. I had a good day yesterday but woke up at 5 AM today in a panic. I'd had a weird dream and decided to just start the day early. The dream wasn't that bad, but I was afraid that I couldn't trust my intuition based on it. I also worried that all of the positive things that I experienced yesterday weren't real. I felt this need to heal my brain but was unsure about my intuition. Maybe it was just a fear or biological response to the fact that this whole thing has been going on nonstop for years. I decided that I must retrain my brain. During my meditation, I felt like I was getting answers to my questions, and that's what meditation is supposed to be.

I focused on connecting with Miah. Saying good morning to her, I intuitively looked up, but didn't actually see her. I had to imagine her, but I felt her. When I asked her where Reggie was, she told me that Reggie loves me. I smiled, satisfied with our interaction, but still felt some panic related to the dream I'd had.

So, I got on the treadmill and attempted to walk off the panic. It had been a bad night's sleep and I always try to guard my sleep. Bundy had caused some of it last night because he'd been having a really hard time. When he got into bed, he woke me up. Then, at three in the morning, the dog started barking. Next, I had that bad dream. I just couldn't win.

Today, I still sort of felt unsure if I could trust my intuition. I have to learn to differentiate between intuition and anxiety, because I have to be okay with living in the present. And presently, the main priority is to heal my brain, to grieve, and to get my body ready for the next chapter of my life which will involve helping a lot of other people. Still, I know that I must heal myself first. And I know that I have to help my husband. My intuition told me that he might pass away soon because he's been getting tired. I thought about how thankful for him I was. He is a good, loyal man. Bundy has always been there physically, but not always emotionally. He checked out a lot when Reggie was getting sick, but that was the way he coped. Despite that, I would do anything for him.

I thought about how Bundy had spent a lot of time with Reggie. Reggie had been hard since the day he was born. He would never sleep, and Bundy would always get him back to sleep. I thought about how Miah had been Bundy's princess too, his baby girl. My meditation turned into stories and Controlled Grief, but that was okay.

On day fifteen, I was feeling every type of grief including some anticipatory grief for my husband. I think I've honestly been feeling it for a couple of years. It was really a shock that Miah went before him. Miah had been so happy here, although really missing her brother, but I believe that she had some sort of spiritual connection with Reggie while she was still alive. After Reggie died, I felt depression and anxiety, but Miah remained happy and content. She knew that she was safe and did not want to live past her Daddy's death.

With anticipatory grief, sometimes you try to emotionally separate, and I realized that I've been doing that with my husband. That's why the day before, I'd tried to spend time with him, and reconnect. He didn't deserve what was happening to him, to us.

I keep wrestling with God though. But God continues to tell me, "This is your purpose. It's way bigger. You get to be eternally connected to your kids." At the end of my meditation, I decided that it was going to be a good day. It started off rough, but the contemplative time really helped me.

I'd just about finished the grief book that I'd been reading. When I reached out to the author, Mary Francis O'Connor, I got an autoreply. She recommended The Center for Prolonged Grief, so I checked it out. It mentioned that acute, integrated, and complicated grief occurs. Obviously, integrated grief is a result of adapting to the loss. When someone adapts to a loss, the grief is not over. Instead, the thoughts, feelings, and behaviors related to the loss are integrated in ways that allow the person to remember and honor the one who died. Then, grief finds a place in their life.

Complicated grief occurs when something interferes with that adaptation. When that happens, acute grief can persist for a very long period of time. A person with complicated grief feels intense, emotional pain. They can't stop feeling like their loved one might somehow reappear, and they often don't see a pathway forward. A future without the loved one seems like forever. I found the book's content impactful and felt that it aligned, for the most part, with my thoughts around grief.

"You have the power to heal yourself from within."

~ Dr. B

Journal

Use this page to journal any thoughts and feelings you may be experiencing along your journey:

_____

_____

_____

_____

_____

_____

_____

_____

_____

_____

_____

_____

_____

_____

_____

_____

_____

_____

Dr. B's Controlled Grief and 5 SELF's Process Day 15

Controlled Grief: I spent some private time just crying. I wasn't angry. I feel good about my spiritual connection.

- o **Spiritual Self:** I woke up in a panic and then tried to walk it off. Meditation worked.
- o **Self-Improvement:** Nothing specific on this day.
- o **Self-Movement**: I went into a massage with the specific purpose of moving grief from the body.
- o **Self-Regulation/Choose:** I chose to make it a good day.
- o **Self-Care**: I participated in gymnastics.

My Controlled Grief Journey Day 15

Date: / /

What is your mood today?
(circle or fill in your own word)

Open	Loving	Sad	Guilty
Calm	Present	Depressed	Afraid
Relaxed	Safe	Broken Hearted	Overwhelmed
Hopeful	Angry	Irritable	Exhausted
Connected	Furious	Longing	Drained
Strong	Resentful	Disconnected	Numb

What activity did you choose to practice for **Controlled Grief**? _____

_____

What have you done today to empower your **Spiritual Self**? _____

_____

How did you practice **Self-Regulation** today? _____

_____

How were you able to work on **Self-Improvement** today? _____

_____

How were you able to prioritize your **Self-Care**? _____

_____

How were you able to work on **Self-Movement** today? _____

_____

Any other thoughts you want to remember about your **journey** today?

_____

Choice Opportunity of the day:
For Day 15, I want you to research another grief theory. Again, figure out what you can relate to (or not) by using this same worksheet.

Choice Opportunity: Process using Grief Theories

 Use the Mentally STRONG Grief series or an internet search. Choose one or more grief theories. Study and/or meditate on the concepts of the grief theory.

Sample list of grief theories to get you started, various theorists:

- 5 Stages of Grief
- Dialectical Thinking in Grief
- Moving Through Grief
- Grow Around Your Grief
- 4 Tasks of Grief
- Physical Impact of Grief
- The 6 R's of Mourning

- The Dual Process Model of Grief
- Grief Work Theory
- The Grieving Brain
- Grief and Attachment
- Continuing Bonds
- Trajectories of Grief
- Find your own

In your own words, describe the grief theory that you chose:

_____

_____

_____

_____

Acknowledge any triggers or negative responses. For example, "that's not how I feel", "it's not that easy", or "I can never accept this".

_____

_____

_____

Now reframe or minimize the above negative statements. For example: "Acceptance doesn't have to mean it's okay, it can be an acknowledgement of the pain, even if that pain is there for the rest of your life." Write your reframed positive statement below:

_____

_____

What did you learn from this grief theory?

_____

_____

_____

_____

Based on your personal grief journey, what criticisms do you have of this grief theory?

_____

_____

_____

_____

What is your personal take away from studying this grief theory? For example: coping strategies, interventions, change in mindset, or grace given to yourself.

_____

_____

_____

_____

This is your Choice Opportunity to be  Mentally STRONG® in learning about grief.

Learn more about *The Mentally STRONG Method*: 1-800-55-STRONG ~ www.mentallystrong.com

Theme: I am enough.
Mood: Overwhelm followed by acknowledgment.

I am having a hard time in the mornings. I often wake up sad and have trouble finding motivation. Documenting everything has me a bit overwhelmed too, so I've decided that I have to manage expectations of myself. Maybe it's because I have a Type A personality and get anxiety around not doing enough. It's so evident in all areas of my life and the fact that I've neglected my self-care validates it further.

At one point, I felt negative thoughts overwhelming me, so I reached out to my sister. She's always been a great support system for me. We talked about everything that I've been feeling and experiencing. Together we decided that my feelings were related to my core connection which is the feeling that "I am not enough." These feelings stem way back to my childhood experiences. On days like these, I have to remind myself that I am enough, and that I did enough for everyone who needed me, particularly my children.

I must manage my expectations of myself during these 45 days of grief. It's hard to put yourself into this space of grief every single day, yet here I am, day after day. Talking with my sister gave me just the energy I needed to continue on with my journey and helped to put me in a better frame of mind. It's important to know who to reach out to, and who you can talk to when you need that extra push. My sister is that person for me.

Dr. B's Controlled Grief and 5 SELF's Process Day 16

Controlled Grief: I called my sister when I was flooded with negative thoughts.

- o **Spiritual Self:** Miah kept reminding me, "I'm right here mommy."
- o **Self-Improvement**: I continued to read *The Grieving Brain*.
- o **Self-Movement**: I walked and worked on the treadmill.
- o **Self-Regulation/Choose:** I dealt with my core connection and feeling that "I am not enough."
- o **Self-Care:** Behaviors and choices: HBOT (hyperbaric oxygen therapy) to address physical health.

My Controlled Grief Journey Day 16

Date: ___/___/___

What is your mood today?
(circle or fill in your own word)

Open	Loving	Sad	Guilty
Calm	Present	Depressed	Afraid
Relaxed	Safe	Broken Hearted	Overwhelmed
Hopeful	Angry	Irritable	Exhausted
Connected	Furious	Longing	Drained
Strong	Resentful	Disconnected	Numb

What activity did you choose to practice for **Controlled Grief**? _____

_____

What have you done today to empower your **Spiritual Self**? _____

_____

How did you practice **Self-Regulation** today? _____

_____

How were you able to work on **Self-Improvement** today? _____

_____

How were you able to prioritize your **Self-Care**? _____

_____

How were you able to work on **Self-Movement** today? _____

_____

Any other thoughts you want to remember about your **journey** today?

_____

Choice Opportunity of the day:

If you're just getting into the thick of your grief, you must manage your expectations around grief. It can be so heavy and intense. There are so many layers in terms of how you manage your expectations in grief. That's why I chose today's Choice Opportunity.

Choice Opportunity: Managing Expectations in Grief

Actively grieving takes mental energy as well as physical energy. It is important to understand grief is not one single emotion but a powerful response we experience following a personally painful or traumatic event. Therefore, managing your responsibilities and expectations will allow time to properly grieve.

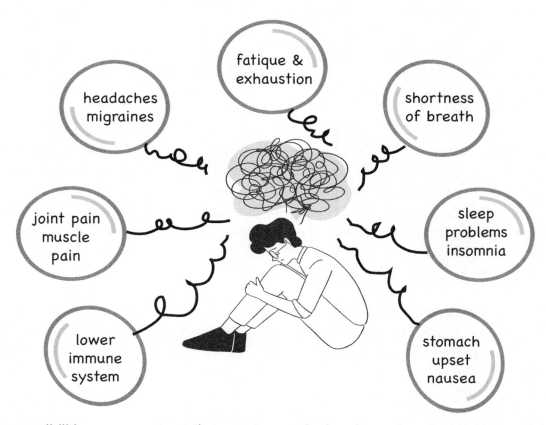

List the responsibilities you must continue as you actively grieve. Consider which activities you can decrease your time commitment and circle them.

_____

_____

_____

_____

_____

_____

Do you have friends/family who can offer support? You may need to explain to them your need to slow down. If possible ask for help with some of your responsibilites. Taking care of yourself and listening to your body is important during this time of grief. This is not the time to take on ANY new activity or responsibilities.

This is your Choice Opportunity to be

Day 17 – Dr. B's Experience

Theme: Processing.
Mood: It's not okay, but I am okay.

Morning is always the hardest time for me because I wake up and realize my reality. My depression feels like a weight. It feels like fatigue. I feel that it's okay to be alone with my thoughts, but it's not great.

During my meditation, I reflected on the tipping point of my grief which was Johnny's death. It was such a dark moment after things had been going so well in my life. The tragedy appeared out of nowhere and was a catalyst for the shift in how I feel about myself. After it occurred, I began to doubt myself and my abilities. Before Johnny's death, I felt like I knew what my purpose was and believed that my family would continue to be blessed. Johnny's death dashed my plans and was my first encounter with grief. At the time, I didn't understand how much more I would be experiencing. Now, I have the complete picture.

Right after Johnny's death, I felt like I was living in a tunnel for a while, a lot of dark spaces. I remember the day he drowned, watching everything happen. Standing on the bank of the river, everyone was praying that we'd find him. The rescue divers were in the water looking frantically. As a nurse, I knew that he was already dead. He'd been under the water for too long. And so, I just stood there in shock, not sure what to do, powerless. I watched everyone from what seemed like a tunnel. I let them take care of all of the details because I just wanted to run away. We were not at home, though, and I really wanted to go home. But home was a 16-hour drive so there was no way I could get there quickly. I remember this intense pain in the back of my shoulders and the sorrow that surrounded me and filled my heart.

When I finally got back to our house after the drowning, I tried to figure out what to do. Those days are a blur to me now. It's almost like I blocked out Johnny's whole memorial, perhaps because of the shock. We'd put up a big poster of Johnny at the event which Cristina eventually moved to her room. She had it there for a long time, and I can still picture it hanging on the wall now.

At the time of Johnny's death, it was almost like I didn't ever really process it because other things kept happening that I had to respond to instead. I was a mother of six and there was always something to do. I kept telling myself that I could get through it and that everything was going to be okay, but then more bad things continued to happen, and I doubted myself. That doubt lingers to this day.

During my Controlled Grief session in the afternoon, I tried to answer what it was like to be in the present moment. Painful, fearful, and mentally tiring. I asked myself questions that were meant to help me remember my children. I didn't need any help with that, though. I thought about their laughs and how they looked. I reminisced about our vacations and where we liked to go. We had many amazing trips to Disney, SeaWorld, and Universal Studios.

I asked myself what they loved above all else. I figured that the answer must be me. They loved their momma. What always stood out to me about them was Miah's love, Johnny's quiet power, and Reggie's energy. I recalled that energy, power, and love. I try to tap into it when I need to but continue to notice the emptiness left by the people I've lost. Unfortunately, I have been living in that emptiness to a large extent.

My grief feels like a spiritual awakening, and a tug of war in my brain. I'm working through some things and have felt Reggie and Miah's presence. I acknowledge how beautiful the time that I had with them was and all that I learned. They made me who I am. But then I feel sorrow and anger. There's also depression and hopelessness for me, although I am trying to pull away from that.

Later on, I had a Mentally STRONG counseling session. My counselor asked me, "How do you think you're coping?" I told her that I'm doing the best that I can. I don't think there is anything that my friends and family can do to help. It's on me. My counselor suggested an outlet for processing my emotions like painting, singing, cooking, or thinking through it all. I have been thinking a lot (I'm definitely not a singer or cook) and working to identify my negative thoughts. For example, sometimes I feel that I am not a good mother, or that I am not a mother anymore. I admitted to my Mentally STRONG counselor that I've also started feeling like no one really loves me. As my counselor reminded me (and as I also know), these feelings are just negative internal dialogue, and not the truth.

As we continued on with the session, I mentioned that I've been updating my house which has been a trigger for me because I have always tried to make my house a home- adopting children and including people that I love in gatherings there. In the next season of my life, I'm going to be alone in that house. I mean, I have support and I'm not totally by myself, but my life will be much more independent. Love makes a house a home and I don't know if I'll have anyone else to love. What I do hope to have in the future is travel, influence, and adventure. My goals have changed as a result of my grief. My counselor and I talked through that.

Journal

"You can choose to be Mentally STRONG" ~ Dr. B

Use this page to journal any thoughts and feelings you may be experiencing along your journey:

_____

_____

_____

_____

_____

_____

_____

_____

_____

_____

_____

_____

_____

_____

_____

_____

_____

_____

_____

As we discussed, I have a choice in all of this. I can choose to heal, to take care of myself, and to find the good in the next chapter of my life, the next season. It's going to be completely different, and I often feel sad when I think about memories of what once was. It's never going to be okay, but I can be okay.

I think one of the things that I told my sister, probably a year and a half ago is that if something ever happened to Miah (after having lost Johnny and Reggie already), watch me because I might kill myself. It's been ten and a half months since Miah's death, and I am not going to kill myself. I'm certain of that. So, what I learned about myself is that I can handle literally anything. The absolute worst has happened to me more than once. And it hurts, but I'm going to be okay. It is possible to transform pain into remembrance, and grief into purpose, and that's my plan.

Dr. B's Controlled Grief and 5 SELF's Process Day 17

Controlled Grief: I went through an entire book on grief.

- **Spiritual Self**: Meditating and praying on the shift that happened to me during Johnny's death.
- **Self-Improvement***:* I read the *F**k Death* book.
- **Self-Movement**: I was brain spotting and processing the whole day.
- **Self-Regulation/Choose:** I spend time addressing negative thoughts.
- **Self-Care:** I participated in skin care and HBOT.

My Controlled Grief Journey Day 17

Date: /   /

What is your mood today?
(circle or fill in your own word)

Open	Loving	Sad	Guilty
Calm	Present	Depressed	Afraid
Relaxed	Safe	Broken Hearted	Overwhelmed
Hopeful	Angry	Irritable	Exhausted
Connected	Furious	Longing	Drained
Strong	Resentful	Disconnected	Numb

What activity did you choose to practice for **Controlled Grief**? _____

_____

What have you done today to empower your **Spiritual Self**? _____

_____

How did you practice **Self-Regulation** today? _____

_____

How were you able to work on **Self-Improvement** today? _____

_____

How were you able to prioritize your **Self-Care**? _____

_____

How were you able to work on **Self-Movement** today? _____

_____

Any other thoughts you want to remember about your **journey** today?

_____

Choice Opportunity of the day:

Day 17 was an intense day for me, and I realized many people who have experienced intense grief seriously consider suicide. I want you to take a moment right now and decide that you will never choose to kill yourself. Feeling suicidal is a feeling, but it does not have to be an action. Please commit to never hurting yourself; this is between you, your God, and the universe. It's not for anyone else to decide so please take this commitment seriously.

Choice Opportunity: #NOTANOPTION

You have a CHOICE. Choose and Decide today that suicide is NOT AN OPTION.

I,_____, agree that suicide is **not an option**. I will not attempt suicide or harm myself in any way.

I agree that I will take the following actions if I am ever suicidal:

1) I will remind myself of my contract that I can never attempt suicide or harm myself in any way.

2) I will call 911 if I believe that I am in immediate danger of harming myself.

3) I will call any or all the following people if I am not in immediate danger of harming myself but have suicidal thoughts:

_____

_____

_____

1-800-SUICIDE

Signed:_____Date:_____

You ARE Mentally STRONG!

Learn more about *The Mentally STRONG Method*: **1-800-55-STRONG ~ www.mentallystrong.com**

Journal

Use this page to journal any thoughts and feelings you may be experiencing along your journey:

Day 18 - Dr. B's Experience

Theme: Embracing my new identity.
Mood: Sorrow followed by reflection.

Day 18 for me was evidence in terms of why I really want people to find consecutive days that they can go through this process. As you start to unravel the layers of your grief and the impact that it's had on your life, you get to a point where you start to question what's next. That was day eighteen for me. I began asking myself, who am I without my children? My identity for so long has been wrapped around the fact that I adopted five children and had two biological children. But I lost one adopted child and both of my biological children, and my other adopted children are now grown. That leaves me without any children in my home, and unsure of who I am now.

As they say, the love that you have for your children is the most intense, genuine love that there is. Because I lost my biological children, I begin to wonder if I am even still a mother now. If not, who am I? I'm not the same person I was before I had kids and I'm not the same person that I was when they were alive. Today, I came to the acknowledgment that I must figure out who I am now (without my children), and I am committed to doing just that.

Dr. B's Controlled Grief and 5 SELF's Process Day 18

Controlled Grief: Trying to practice Controlled Grief and not have it impact my mood.

- **Spiritual Self:** Who am I without my attachments?
- **Self-Improvement:** My self-improvement is ongoing.
- **Self-Regulation:** My mood was impacted by my grief today.
- **Self-Movement:** I walked on the treadmill and did gymnastics.
- **Self-Care:** I love gymnastics, so it is a form of self-care for me.

My Controlled Grief Journey Day 18

Date: /   /

What is your mood today?
(circle or fill in your own word)

Open	Loving	Sad	Guilty
Calm	Present	Depressed	Afraid
Relaxed	Safe	Broken Hearted	Overwhelmed
Hopeful	Angry	Irritable	Exhausted
Connected	Furious	Longing	Drained
Strong	Resentful	Disconnected	Numb

What activity did you choose to practice for **Controlled Grief**? _____

_____

What have you done today to empower your **Spiritual Self**? _____

_____

How did you practice **Self-Regulation** today? _____

_____

How were you able to work on **Self-Improvement** today? _____

_____

How were you able to prioritize your **Self-Care**? _____

_____

How were you able to work on **Self-Movement** today? _____

_____

Any other thoughts you want to remember about your **journey** today?

_____

Choice Opportunity of the day:

As I was working through the layers on Day 18, I realized that it boiled down to *Who am I?* Who am I without my children? Who am I in general? That's why I chose this Choice Opportunity for you because there is a change of identity that accompanies loss.

Choice Opportunity: Who Am I?

Expected outcome: Gain knowledge and insight of one's purpose and in an attempt to define themselves.

Knowing who you are, what you want, and where you want to go is important in fulfilling your purpose in your life. The following questions can help you to discover who you are, what you want, and where you want to go.

1. I like myself because:

_____

_____

2. I feel good about:

_____

_____

3. My friends would say that I have a great:

_____

_____

4. I am loved by:

_____

_____

5. People say I am good at:

_____

_____

6. Five positive things others say about me:

_____

_____

7. I consider myself a good:

_____

_____

Learn more about *The Mentally STRONG Method*: 1-800-55-STRONG ~ www.mentallystrong.com

*The Mentally STRONG Method with Choice Opportunities© Author: Cristi Bundukamara – not for reproduction/distribution

8. I have overcome:

_____

_____

9. I enjoy doing:

_____

_____

10. I know I will attain my personal vision, because I am:

_____

_____

11. People compliment me about:

_____

_____

12. I feel good when:

_____

_____

13. I've been successful at:

_____

_____

14. I laugh when I think about:

_____

_____

15. The traits I admire about myself are:

_____

_____

16. I think positively about myself when:

_____

_____

Day 19 - Dr. B's Experience

Theme: Balance between manifesting positive things and acknowledging grief and trauma.

Mood: Forward thinking while setting my personal visions.

On Day 19, I continued to focus on figuring out who I am now. I chose to work on some personal visions which are part of the Mentally Strong Method that I've created (see Appendix A for more information). A lot of Self-Help books talk about knowing who you want to be, what you want to be, and what you want to attain. You are not going to get anywhere if you don't know where you're trying to go. So, to this end, I worked on my Personal Visions today. One was around my health because I found out that I had some neuro inflammation and problems that were causing decreased profusion to my brain.

Part of that health-related Personal Vision has to do with taking care of my systems by going to the doctor, following up on all abnormal lab tests, and incorporating new diet and lifestyle routines. Being healthier will help me with where I am in my life now. The overarching personal vision for me is to get a handle on my health and to figure out what's good for me and what's not. I am committed to making choices that are good for me henceforth.

I decided that I also need a Personal Vision regarding my professional success. I've been talking about wanting to turn my pain into purpose. Going through this grief process has been helpful for me, but how do I parlay that into genuine care and help for others while still maintaining my mental and emotional health?

My last Personal Vision has to do with my spiritual connection. I am open to whatever God has in store for me, but I continue to struggle with the fundamental biblical teaching that was engrained in me. Overall, I want to stay true to it while continuing to grow spiritually.

"Feeling the pain can ultimately provide healing"
~ Dr. B

Use this page to journal any thoughts and feelings you may be experiencing along your journey:

_____

_____

_____

_____

_____

_____

_____

_____

_____

_____

_____

_____

_____

_____

_____

_____

_____

_____

_____

_____

Dr. B's Controlled Grief and 5 SELF's Process Day 19

Controlled Grief: I looked through pictures of Miah on my computer.

- o **Spiritual Self:** My meditation involved creating the energy for the day.
- o **Self-Improvement:** I read the book: *The Body Keeps The Score*
- o **Self-Movement:** I walked on the treadmill.
- o **Self-Regulation/Choose:** Question - what is trauma? I worked on three personal visions: Health, Professional Success, and Spiritual Connection.
- o **Self-Care:** I did my HBOT and set up some medical appointments.

My Controlled Grief Journey Day 19

Date: /   /

What is your mood today?

(circle or fill in your own word)

Open	Loving	Sad	Guilty
Calm	Present	Depressed	Afraid
Relaxed	Safe	Broken Hearted	Overwhelmed
Hopeful	Angry	Irritable	Exhausted
Connected	Furious	Longing	Drained
Strong	Resentful	Disconnected	Numb

What activity did you choose to practice for **Controlled Grief**? _____

_____

What have you done today to empower your **Spiritual Self**? _____

_____

How did you practice **Self-Regulation** today? _____

_____

How were you able to work on **Self-Improvement** today? _____

_____

How were you able to prioritize your **Self-Care**? _____

_____

How were you able to work on **Self-Movement** today? _____

_____

Any other thoughts you want to remember about your **journey** today?

_____

Choice Opportunity of the day:

After you work through deciding who you are, it's time to develop a Personal Vision related to who you want to be. It's not just about career or body type or that kind of thing. It involves what type of person you want to be in the future (looking ahead). That's why for Day 19's Choice Opportunity, you will work on some Personal Visions around that.

Choice Opportunity: Developing Your Personal Vision

Expected Outcome: Start working on developing your personal visions. This is only the first step in the Personal Vision element.

Choose a category below and brainstorm ideas of what you want your Personal Vision to look like. This can change over time.

Physical ☐   Financial ☐   Intelligence ☐

Mental ☐   Career ☐   Lifestyle ☐

Emotional ☐   Purpose ☐   Sobriety ☐

Spiritual ☐   Relationships ☐   Other ☐

Faith ☐   Family ☐

How to create your Personal Vision:	Your Turn! Write your Personal Vision in this box:
Think of this as your ultimate vision for your life. Think BIG. *Example: Emotional Personal Vision – I want to have insight and control over my emotions.*	
What obstacles are trying to hold me back from obtaining this Personal Vision: Obstacle or Barrier: A thing that blocks one's way or prevents or hinders progress. *Example: I don't know why I'm so sensitive.*	**Your Turn!** Write your obstacles to your Personal Vision in this box:

Learn more about *The Mentally STRONG Method*: 1-800-55-STRONG ~ www.mentallystrong.com

*The Mentally STRONG Method with Choice Opportunities© Author: Cristi Bundukamara – not for reproduction/distribution

What can I do RIGHT NOW: This is where you can come up with small actionable steps that can bring you closer to your Personal Vision right now. *Example: Work through a Thought Map around my sensitivity.*	**Your Turn!** What small action can you take right now to bring you closer to your Personal Vision?:
Action Plan: **Next you will create an action plan for yourself for the short and long term.** *Example:* *Schedule weekly time to go through The Mentally STRONG Method* *Journal my thoughts and feelings daily*	**Your Turn!** Next, create an action plan for the short and long term below:

This is your *Choice Opportunity* to be   Mentally STRONG® in Personal Vision!

Learn more about *The Mentally STRONG Method*: **1-800-55-STRONG ~** www.mentallystrong.com

*The Mentally STRONG Method with Choice Opportunities© Author: Cristi Bundukamara – not for reproduction/distribution

Day 20 – Dr. B's Experience

Theme: Learning to be present.
Mood: What's next?

I began my morning meditation with the intention to receive. Issues related to my brain health were heavy on my mind. I also thought about the last 15 years of my life and what the next chapter would hold. There are already so many things that I'm proud of including accomplishments, internal work, and who I've become. The things that I'm grateful for, however, are not enough, and the grief creeps into every meditation. The bright spot that persists despite it, though, is that I have been able to feel an eternal spiritual connection to my children.

The more I learn from all of this, the more I realize all that I don't know. I've always been the kind of person that wants to figure out what the right answer is. In fact, I want to know everything, but we can't know everything, obviously. I realize that the spiritual dimension is vast. My relationships with God, my children, and other people here on Earth are also vast. If I'm trusting my intuition, I feel like I'm going to live a long time. It's been 11 months without Miah and six years without Reggie. And it's been over 10 years without my grown children actively in my life. I've been living alone with this anticipatory uncomfortableness about my husband and his DRPLA progression. Still, I've been trying to receive and plan what I am supposed to do next. I realize that I'll probably have to sit in my current reality a little while longer.

I look at this moment as a time for healing. I have to heal from my many years of fight or flight, so that I can be present. I've never truly been present. I'm always pushing through and moving forward, trying to make the best of every moment. Now, I want to learn how to be present in a non-stressful way.

My kids had an amazing life. It always made me happy to make them happy, but what now? Yes, there's going to be a purpose and I'm going to help lots of people, but what makes *me* happy? I'm important too. Why is it so painful to find my own happiness? I guess when I really drill down on it, it's because I don't want to be alone. People and connections make me happy. So, I pray that God brings more of those connections around. No matter what, I'm going to be okay.

I went into my Controlled Grief session today and Reggie's toys just kind of surrounded me. Overwhelmed and slightly discouraged, I was fighting off a little bit of a headache. I feel connected to Reggie and Miah but am not sure where to go from here. How do I have true, meaningful connections with people? One of the things that I started doing in this process, and I think it's important for everybody, is to really begin taking care of myself. I'm finally addressing some medical issues that I've ignored for a long time.

Another thing that I'm trying to learn is how to be present and happy in the moment. I don't know how to do that yet. I've been running my whole life chasing after the next goal, the next dream, or the next person to save. I have been so busy that I haven't actually stopped to make sure that I am well myself. In the past, I was distracted by taking care of my children. I'm now trying to make that shift towards Self-Care.

Who am I without helping my children though? Who am I without a disease to fight? I've been holding my breath for so long. There were so many good times in the midst of all of that tragedy, but I'm still in this mode where I'm waiting for the next bad thing to happen.

It is comforting to know that grief symptoms occur for everyone. Which symptoms am I experiencing? I'm unable to concentrate and I don't want to go anywhere. Maybe I kind of want to go, but I don't want to plan it. And if it's cold outside (which it often is in Colorado), then I don't feel like going through the extra effort at all. I also feel angry and irritable, like nothing interests me. I've worked through some of those feelings, but I'm upset that the rest of the world goes on as normal while my own world has been shattered.

I feel like I've worked through a lot of my anger, but then I'll hear a song and cry, and it will come back again. Today, I remembered how Miah was upset with me because I didn't wake her up to say goodbye to Reggie before he died. I thought she would be better off to stay sleeping, but it is always best to get our goodbyes in when we can. I realize that now.

Although I am moving forward and holding my head high, I do still really struggle at times. First thing in the morning is particularly hard for me. There is this persistent fear of what's coming next; related to my health and my husbands too. That's why it's crucial that I continue to process my grief and do my best to learn how to be present. I have to enjoy the moments that I have left with Bundy and appreciate my health.

Dr. B's Controlled Grief and 5 SELF's Process Day 20

Controlled Grief: I sat in Miah and Reggie's room.

- o **Spiritual Self:** What's next? I sat in silence to receive.
- o **Self-Improvement:** I continued to read the book: *The Body Keeps The Score.*
- o **Self-Movement:** Nothing specific on this day.
- o **Self-Regulation/Choose**: I chose to follow up and submit to whatever testing I need to do.
- o **Self-Care:** I got my thyroid ultrasound. Miah said that I would never have taken care of myself as long as she was alive. She didn't know that when she chose to transition, but she knows that now.

My Controlled Grief Journey Day 20

Date: / /

What is your mood today?
(circle or fill in your own word)

Open	Loving	Sad	Guilty
Calm	Present	Depressed	Afraid
Relaxed	Safe	Broken Hearted	Overwhelmed
Hopeful	Angry	Irritable	Exhausted
Connected	Furious	Longing	Drained
Strong	Resentful	Disconnected	Numb

What activity did you choose to practice for **Controlled Grief**? _____

_____

What have you done today to empower your **Spiritual Self**? _____

_____

How did you practice **Self-Regulation** today? _____

_____

How were you able to work on **Self-Improvement** today? _____

_____

How were you able to prioritize your **Self-Care**? _____

_____

How were you able to work on **Self-Movement** today? _____

_____

Any other thoughts you want to remember about your **journey** today?

_____

Choice Opportunity of the day:

For Day 20, you will reflect upon your experience (and future expectations) related to your grief journey thus far. While grieving, it's important to look backward and ahead while identifying key takeaways and areas for deeper reflection. This journal activity will afford you the opportunity to do so.

Writing out our losses is a method of therapy. It will help you connect with your loved one as well as developing resilience. You may want to get a notebook or journal and set aside 20 minutes either daily, weekly, or once a month to spend time telling the stories of life together. While writing the memories you can work through the pain of your loss. Trust your intuition and listen for answers.

Journal Meditations

Before you begin each journal topic, jot down three words which describe how you're feeling right now.

1.	2.	3.

Journal Prompts:

1. If I could talk to you again, I'd tell you . . .

2. One of my fondest memories of you is . . .

3. I am angry with you about . . .

4. I wish I had told you . . .

5. One of my least favorite memories of you is . . .

6. Questions I have for you . . .

7. You made me laugh when . . .

8. What my life may be six months from now . . .

When you finish writing, jot down three words which describe your present feelings.

1.	2.	3.

This is your Choice Opportunity to be Mentally STRONG®

Learn more about *The Mentally STRONG Method*: 1-800-55-STRONG ~ www.mentallystrong.com

Day 21 - Dr. B's Experience

Theme: We don't need to have everything figured out.
Mood: Angry, confused.

This morning, I tried to mentally and emotionally prepare for a grief yoga session, but it was challenging. When I got there, there were a couple of people supporting me which was nice, but I wanted it to be more of a meditative practice to release some of my grief (more than I wanted it to be a social experience). Although I have been at this for some time now, all that keeps coming up for me this morning is still anger and this yoga session was no exception. So, I decided to get back to the punching bag. I don't even know what I'm angry about this morning, but it's probably injustices. Things are just not fair. There was a mass shooting in our town last night, and there is so much grief and anger all around. And that anger and grief is coming towards me. I don't like pain that doesn't make sense, and that the same people have to go through so much. It's like what happened with my adopted kids who experienced so much trauma before joining our family, and then after that, they had to deal with so much more (losing three siblings). Why?

For that matter, why did I have to lose three kids? Johnny first, and then both Reggie and Miah. I mean, it's hard to lose one, but three, that is so far from fair. I don't like hitting this bag, or anything, but I'm upset. I am mad about waiting, patience, and expectations; expectations of me, and of God. God wants people to love Him but continues to take everything because of that expectation. That's not fair.

The mass shooting today in my hometown brings up some anger that I have towards God. All the hate saddens me so much. Adding to that is the fact that I don't personally have a story of God loving me. God is complicated. This grief is so challenging, and the anger takes so much mental energy to get through.

I wish that God could take some of it away (the grief, the anger), but I am left to take care of myself. Taking care of myself is not intuitive and I have a hard time finding joy. Then, I have God's expectations of me. I started thinking about that saying, "God doesn't give you anything more than you can handle." At what point do you say "no" to that, though? At what point? I'm never going to figure it out.

We don't get to know why. Sure, I'm going to try to turn my pain into purpose and help other people. But I'm using so much mental energy trying to figure everything out. Maybe there's nothing to figure out. My children are gone, and this anger is not healthy. I must attempt to get rid of it, and this process of actively engaging in my grief is helping me.

Dr. B's Controlled Grief and 5 SELF's Process Day 21

Controlled Grief: Working through my anger with God about losing my children in preparation for my grief yoga.

- o **Spiritual Self:** The mass shooting brings up so much anger directed at God.
- o **Self-Improvement:** Purpose/intention of grief yoga: connect to the divine and find joy.
- o **Self-Movement:** I participated in grief yoga.
- o **Self-Regulation/Choose:** I separated my spiritual conflict and injustice from my grief to receive from the grief yoga session.
- o **Self-Care:** I spend time with people during grief yoga and being social afterwards.

My Controlled Grief Journey Day 21

Date: /   /

What is your mood today?
(circle or fill in your own word)

Open	Loving	Sad	Guilty
Calm	Present	Depressed	Afraid
Relaxed	Safe	Broken Hearted	Overwhelmed
Hopeful	Angry	Irritable	Exhausted
Connected	Furious	Longing	Drained
Strong	Resentful	Disconnected	Numb

What activity did you choose to practice for **Controlled Grief**? _____

_____

What have you done today to empower your **Spiritual Self**? _____

_____

How did you practice **Self-Regulation** today? _____

_____

How were you able to work on **Self-Improvement** today? _____

_____

How were you able to prioritize your **Self-Care**? _____

_____

How were you able to work on **Self-Movement** today? _____

_____

Any other thoughts you want to remember about your **journey** today?

_____

Choice Opportunity of the day:

I chose the Choice Opportunity for Day 21 as an activity to release some of your pain and anger. You can beat the anger, burn it, or break it up sometimes. I put sticky notes (that list the things I'm mad about) on a punching bag before I punch it sometimes. When I'm done, I burn those sticky notes (further releasing the anger). I have purposely broken things before as part of this process. All of these activities are okay as a way to release pain and can be a useful part of the Controlled Grief process. Just be careful!

For some people the only way to release anger is to exhibit physical aggression to self, others, or property. If you find yourself choosing to hurt yourself, breaking things, lashing out at others, or even just being easily irritated you might benefit from a physical activity that demonstrates your anger.

beat ● burn ● break

Directions:

Identify specifically what or who you are angry at.

List each item on a separate piece of paper.

Explain the reason for your anger.

Choose a physical action against the piece(s) of paper.

☐ Tape the pieces of paper on a punching bag, then punch it.

☐ Burn the pieces of paper, in a safe manner.

☐ Rip each piece into tiny pieces.

☐ Or do all three!

Repeat if necessary.

This is your Choice Opportunity to be Mentally STRONG®

Learn more about *The Mentally STRONG Method*: 1-800-55-STRONG ~ www.mentallystrong.com

Day 22 – Dr. B's Experience

Theme: My voice and experience matter.
Mood: Be there for others but still take care of myself.

My meditation for today was about processing yesterday's grief and the weekend's activities. When I went into grief yoga yesterday, I was very anxious. I don't know why because I do yoga a lot, and I was with my close friends. Perhaps it's because I feel like there's this expectation that when we do something, that we're all going to feel better. But I don't truly know if everyone will feel better although I hope for the best.

Controlled Grief is about taking the time, feeling the pain, bringing it to the surface and then processing it. I'm on Day 22, and I'm doing it every day. I do feel the healing, but some of it is never going to leave me. So, because I was going into yoga anxiously, I decided to deal with that anxiety head on and cried. When I engage in it actively, it brings many things up, but it doesn't actually make the anxiety lessen.

As a result, I started off the session a little overly emotional, and a little disappointed. I thought that the yoga instructor would feed into my grief/anxiety to bring it out, but she didn't, which was actually really good. She stated that her intention was to bring joy to the surface, to ground us, and to help us come to understand that grief is a part of life. I have to admit that when she said it sometimes, it was a trigger for me. Losing your kids should not be a part of life. But, if we truly believe that our soul is eternal, and I do, it means that our soul never dies. Even the most heinous grief, like losing a child, is still part of this life. By the end of the grief yoga, which was very gentle and grounding, I felt better.

One thing that the instructor talked about was that we all have a spot on our sternum that is tender to grief. I didn't know that before getting my piercing there, but I remember when I got the piercing, I felt broken hearted. I'm still waiting for Reggie and Miah's diamond (made from their ashes) to arrive so that I can attach it to the piercing there. For now, whenever I want to embrace my pain, I can push that tender spot and feel my broken heart. I didn't want to do it today, though, because I wanted to meditate, receive, and have a productive day. And either way, it's okay to feel pain or not, and that's important to realize.

As I'm going through this process and trying to help others, I know that grief feels unbearable to everyone. But I've been thinking a lot lately about what creates a long-term struggle, that's different. It's what professionals call complicated grief or prolonged grief disorder. In involves more: the trauma not being dealt with as trauma, negative self-talk, and maladaptive coping. You have to separate those things and really learn to take care of yourself.

I just worked on a personal vision this morning: Who am I? Who I am is something that I get to decide. I am still a mother, but that's not my responsibility right now. I am also fortunate. Fortunate enough to be in a season where I am able to take care of myself. I encourage you to do that as well.

As I go into meditation this morning, my posture and position are not super important, but unfortunately, I am feeling like I am not able to receive due to the distractions of the world. I hear my phone going off in the other room. My dog is moving around upstairs. I have a little bit of a headache, but I don't want to give into the distractions because I really need to be present for other people today.

That is my choice; to be present for those impacted by the mass shooting. I asked God to help me receive so that I can be present, and to help me put up emotional boundaries so that other people's grief does not trigger my own. I want to be present for others, while taking care of myself.

I was going to try to push through today and not eat breakfast but was told that in order to be present for others, that I must take care of myself. So, I decided to get some food in me so that I can do that. It's going to be a good week.

Dr. B's Controlled Grief and 5 SELF's Process Day 22

Controlled Grief: I'm still processing my first brain spotting session when I "lost my voice." I mapped it out and it came down to a core belief that "my voice (thoughts, feelings, desires)" doesn't matter.

- o **Spiritual Self:** I asked to receive. My intention was to be present for others after the mass shooting.
- o **Self-Improvement:** I got news of a T4 nodule on my thyroid, so I did research on thyroid cancers.
- o **Self-Movement:** I practiced yoga at home.
- o **Self-Regulation/Choose**: I choose to believe that my voice does matter, and that I must take care of myself to be there for others.
- o **Self-Care**: I celebrated with my sister on her birthday.

My Controlled Grief Journey Day 22

Date: /   /

What is your mood today?
(circle or fill in your own word)

Open	Loving	Sad	Guilty
Calm	Present	Depressed	Afraid
Relaxed	Safe	Broken Hearted	Overwhelmed
Hopeful	Angry	Irritable	Exhausted
Connected	Furious	Longing	Drained
Strong	Resentful	Disconnected	Numb

What activity did you choose to practice for **Controlled Grief**? _____

_____

What have you done today to empower your **Spiritual Self**? _____

_____

How did you practice **Self-Regulation** today? _____

_____

How were you able to work on **Self-Improvement** today? _____

_____

How were you able to prioritize your **Self-Care**? _____

_____

How were you able to work on **Self-Movement** today? _____

_____

Any other thoughts you want to remember about your **journey** today?

_____

Choice Opportunity of the day:

I personally work through dialectical thinking in grief. How can two presumably opposite ideas really coexist? For example, I am so grateful that my children are not suffering anymore and that I had an amazing life with them. At the same time, I'm also angry, hurt and feel hopeless without them. Both are true although they appear to be completely opposite ideas. What are your truths and what's opposite the dialectics that you are struggling with?

Dialectic thoughts/feelings are perceived as contradictory.
Using Dialectical thinking allows you to explore and feel the reality of both truths.

WHERE 2 OPPOSITES CAN COEXIST.

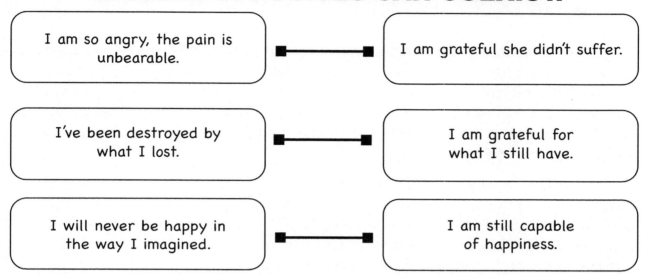

I am so angry, the pain is unbearable.	I am grateful she didn't suffer.
I've been destroyed by what I lost.	I am grateful for what I still have.
I will never be happy in the way I imagined.	I am still capable of happiness.

SIT WITH THE CONTRADICTION - BOTH ARE TRUE

Now, take your two thoughts and merge them into a new statement of truth.

Your emotion/thought:

New statement of truth:

Contradiction:

RECONCILE YOUR THOUGHTS - DON'T REPLACE THEM

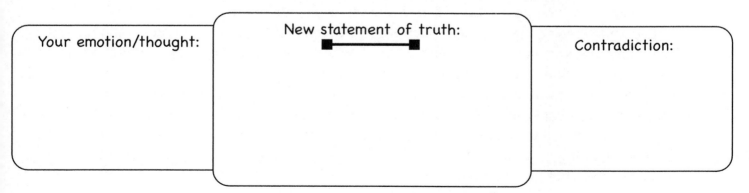

Your emotion/thought:

New statement of truth:

Contradiction:

This is your Choice Opportunity to be   Mentally STRONG®

Learn more about *The Mentally STRONG Method*: 1-800-55-STRONG ~ www.mentallystrong.com

Day 23 – Dr. B's Experience

Theme: Finding my truth and voice after losing my children.
Mood: Connection and validation.

I met with another medium today as part of my Controlled Grief. She opened the session by saying that she taps into my energy and the spirits around me. That's how she obtains her information. When receiving and seeing things, she does her best to translate. Some of the information can be very symbolic and needs interpretation. Other times, it can be more literal as if she's looking at a photograph. Some of it may make sense and some of it may not.

During our interaction, I got a visit from Bundy's Dad followed by Reggie and then Miah. The psychic talked about a lot of different things. For starters, she spoke about how stubborn Bundy's Dad was, and that's the truth. She said that he was there playing with Reggie. Bundy's father apologized for being too hardheaded and argumentative, saying that if he were here now, he would be much kinder. Bundy's dad also told me that he was sorry for all that I've been through and wanted to pass his apologies on to Bundy. He wanted to make things right with Bundy before Bundy passed away.

Then Reggie came in and the psychic said that he was a ball of energy and loved to have a good time. She said it was almost like he had ADHD because he saw so much around him that he wanted to engage with. In that moment, she told me that he had a dog and a bicycle and was doing tricks on it.

Reggie wanted to make sure that I passed along a toy to his friend who was having a hard time, and the psychic said that he also wanted to snuggle with me. Reggie told us that the medication made him woozy at the end and that's why he resisted it. Lastly, Reggie told me that he was pushing me to help others, and to travel to a lot of different places.

Next, Miah came through. She told the psychic that she was taking care of Reggie and cleaning up after him. Miah wanted to tell me that she was sorry. Miah also mentioned that she was encouraging me and pushing me out of bed when I didn't want to do anything (She said that Reggie was too). Next, she commented on my hair as well as her own hair. It was something about my roots which made me laugh. Miah was always one for beauty and taking care of herself. There was a good message in that. She also said that it was okay for me to donate some of her toys; she'd like it if I did. And she encouraged me to hang stockings for Christmas, fill them, and then donate the toys. I decided that I would do it!

What a great hour! I ended that session feeling like everything that I've been doing had been validated. It was special to receive those messages from Reggie and Miah and I was happy to get confirmation of their love and unending presence in my life.

Dr. B's Controlled Grief and 5 SELF's Process Day 23

Controlled Grief: It hit me really hard today that this is my new reality forever. I was acknowledging a "permanent loss."

- **Spiritual Self:** The medium confirmed my connection with the spirit world, but I was overwhelmed with the sadness of my new reality.
- **Self-Improvement:** I researched Bowlby's Attachment Theory.
- **Self-Movement:** I walked on the treadmill.
- **Self-Regulation/Choose:** I went to sleep early to give myself rest. I couldn't do anything else. Processing emotional pain is exhausting.
- **Self-Care:** I did my HBOT.

My Controlled Grief Journey Day 23   Date: /   /

What is your mood today?
(circle or fill in your own word)

Open	Loving	Sad	Guilty
Calm	Present	Depressed	Afraid
Relaxed	Safe	Broken Hearted	Overwhelmed
Hopeful	Angry	Irritable	Exhausted
Connected	Furious	Longing	Drained
Strong	Resentful	Disconnected	Numb

What activity did you choose to practice for **Controlled Grief**? _____

_____

What have you done today to empower your **Spiritual Self**? _____

_____

How did you practice **Self-Regulation** today? _____

_____

How were you able to work on **Self-Improvement** today? _____

_____

How were you able to prioritize your **Self-Care**? _____

_____

How were you able to work on **Self-Movement** today? _____

_____

Any other thoughts you want to remember about your **journey** today?

_____

Choice Opportunity of the day:

Learning to untangle your thoughts is a vital part of this process. I've talked about the layers involved with grief, and the ten categories in the mentally strong method, but how do you actually untangle your thoughts here? For Day 23, I challenge you to work through this worksheet and figure out how capable you are of untangling your thoughts.

Choice Opportunity: Untangle Your Thoughts

When we struggle with deep emotional pain our thoughts tend to get jumbled up in our minds and our hearts. These jumbled up thoughts tend to send us in a spiral of deeper emotional pain. If we can untangle these thoughts we can begin to see clearly and be present.

① **What are the facts of your story?**
Write down the basic facts of the loss or the pain. Include only the details of what is true. Do not add any emotion or thoughts, just the facts.

② **What is your version of the story?**
This step is crucial because this may be the root cause of your additional pain. This is the story you are telling yourself, the "reason" behind the facts. This is our way of trying to understand or make sense of what happened.

③ **Rewrite a new story with the rest of your life.**
When you created your version of the story in step 2 you probably added a bunch of "Why" thoughts. Asking "why" questions adds to the suffering. You will never be able to make sense out of the why. These questions only lead to distorted thoughts of catasphorizing, assumptions and blaming. Why questions only lead to a downward spiral of negative answers and unpleasant and troublesome emotions. Now, try to rewrite your story with questions and thoughts that begin with "how" or "what". The answers to these questions will lead to personal growth and impact your emotional life in the present.

This is your Choice Opportunity to be Mentally STRONG®

Learn more about The *Mentally STRONG Method*: 1-800-55-STRONG ~ www.mentallystrong.com

Day 24 – Dr. B's Experience

Theme: Letting go of limiting beliefs. Embracing a new spiritual outlook.
Mood: Compassion for myself and understanding.

The speed at which I am growing and learning is exhausting, but exciting. Much of my mental work and growth is an internal dialogue. I engaged in a Mentally STRONG Method session as part of my Controlled Grief today. It began with me telling the counselor about my thyroid ultrasound which indicated possible cancer. Dealing with a potential health issue has been very scary and unexpected for me. It has also added a new dimension to my grief journey, causing me to focus more on my own self-care and health.

My counselor asked me to describe myself which was more challenging than I would have thought. I would describe myself as a born-again Christian, but I have grown to become more aware of other truths over the past 15 years. Losing my children has caused some pretty significant spiritual conflict for me, and I've turned to other spiritual outlets for answers. As I've mentioned previously, I've seen a couple of mediums and received confirmations about what I have been experiencing spiritually. That connection is something that I want to work on and become more aware of spiritual connections as a whole.

This has been a transformational journey for me, finding my truth, but I believe what I believe. There is more out there than I previously thought and was taught. I have very dear friends that I love that will adamantly disagree with me and judge me for this stance. One of my friends told me this weekend that the Bible says very clearly that we should not go to mediums.

I've been questioning a lot of things lately. What is truth? Can I trust how I feel? Another thought that has been coming up a lot for me is that I'm not good enough (which is a huge core connection). In my brain spotting session, we started with Johnny's drowning (which is not my biggest trauma, but I feel like everything kind of spiraled from there). And I realized that was the day that I lost my voice. And when I mapped it out, it came up that my voice doesn't matter.

It's kind of odd because I've always been kind of opinionated. My family can't believe that I didn't become a lawyer. But, more recently, I've lost a lot of my opinions because the things that I swore were true turned out not to be true. As an example, God is supposed to be loving and protective. If so, then why did he let bad things happen to us? Cristina, Kayla and Johnny, my adopted children, were a sibling group. When they moved in, they had already experienced significant trauma. I told them that they were finally safe, that they were in a loving home, and that they would be taken care of. Then, in literally less than a year, Johnny died. I lied.

So, you see, my opinions were proven wrong, and I shut down my voice. Maybe now I'm compensating by becoming an influencer and a speaker. My reality today is that everything is gray. Before I was trying to figure out what was black and what was white. When everything is gray, there are no absolutes, and no truth.

But it goes back even further, all the way back to childhood when I was told that my emotions were not important. In Church, they said that God doesn't like emotions. I was also taught that women don't have a voice. So, putting it all together when I mapped it out, I realized that I don't have a voice.

I often wonder how I can find balance with my truth and then be comfortable voicing it because I care what everybody thinks and worry about being judged too. My counselor asked me if it would be easier to come up with my own concrete beliefs. I paused. That's challenging for me because I've been trying to keep my logical and intuitive brains separate. I worry that people will think I'm stupid if I lean into that intuitive side. I've felt that way since the third grade. As I've gotten older, I know that I am intelligent, but have a hard time truly believing it if you know what I mean. I feel that my intelligence is more of an emotional intelligence which some might argue is even better.

My counselor then asked me about my personal mantra. I've been thinking about that a lot lately, trying to come up with a new one. It used to be that I was sassy, sexy, and smart, or just those three words. *Smart* because I figured out in what ways I am intelligent. *Sassy* because I was always told that I would never get anywhere with my attitude. And *Sexy* because I want to love my body. And so, I chose those three words to counteract my negative beliefs about myself.

My counselor asked me what I would do if someone told me that I was stupid or fat today. I would probably defend myself first but then internalize it. I link my negative view regarding my intelligence with not being able to pay attention. Even worse, I link that trait with Reggie and Miah's deaths. Perhaps if I were smarter, I would have been paying more attention and would have been able to prevent them from dying. I beat myself up for not seeing the signs. But if I really talk myself through it, I understand

*"You are
stronger than
you think."
~ Dr. B*

Use this page to journal any thoughts and feelings
you may be experiencing along your journey:

_____

_____

_____

_____

_____

_____

_____

_____

_____

_____

_____

_____

_____

_____

_____

_____

_____

_____

_____

_____

_____

that's not the truth. I am not responsible. I couldn't have done anything to prevent their deaths. It takes a lot of mental energy for me to get there though.

Still, I lean into my faith. I'm currently reestablishing an authentic spiritual connection. I want to have complete trust in God and in my spiritual self. Whether God is a single deity or not is not something that I am super concerned about. I want to focus on the concept of being able to just trust in the fact that there's a greater purpose. Otherwise, what's the point?

Dr. B's Controlled Grief and 5 SELF's Process Day 24

Controlled Grief: I worked on a summary of all that I have learned since starting this journey. I acknowledged that I have PTS(D).

- **Spiritual Self:** I'm still processing "finding my voice" which is a new core connection. Meditation occurs in the HBOT chamber, which is 1 hour 3-4 times per week.
- **Self-Improvement**: I studied Freud's grief work.
- **Self-Regulation:** Realization of all the attachment chemicals and neural pathways that are not connected and confused.
- **Self-Movement:** I walked on the treadmill.
- **Self-Care:** I participated in HBOT, light therapy, and Alpha-Stim.

My Controlled Grief Journey Day 24

What is your mood today?
(circle or fill in your own word)

Open	Loving	Sad	Guilty
Calm	Present	Depressed	Afraid
Relaxed	Safe	Broken Hearted	Overwhelmed
Hopeful	Angry	Irritable	Exhausted
Connected	Furious	Longing	Drained
Strong	Resentful	Disconnected	Numb

What activity did you choose to practice for **Controlled Grief**? _____

_____

What have you done today to empower your **Spiritual Self**? _____

_____

How did you practice **Self-Regulation** today? _____

_____

How were you able to work on **Self-Improvement** today? _____

_____

How were you able to prioritize your **Self-Care**? _____

_____

How were you able to work on **Self-Movement** today? _____

_____

Any other thoughts you want to remember about your **journey** today?

_____

Choice Opportunity of the day:
As I've mentioned, I encourage you to meditate all the time. Do you really know how to meditate? This Choice Opportunity involves one easy acronym that I use but there's all kinds of techniques out there to ensure that you are learning how to meditate in this process.

Choice Opportunity: The RELAX Method of Meditation

This Choice Opportunity is designed as a tool for you to use in active meditation. Think about each item below in preparation.

Recognize

What do you want to bring into consciousness, or into active meditation? It could be a prayer, a request, a concern or something else.

Elevate

Lift the identified to God or your spiritual relationship. Identify your belief system, what or who are you elevating this to?

Listen

Sit in stillness, really allow yourself to stop and listen for a response.

Allow

Allow yourself to receive the answer, expect a response, it may not be an answer to your question. Be open to whatever the response is.

eXecute

What are you going to do with what you received? What choices can you make?

Answer the questions on the back of this worksheet to deepen your insight into your meditation practice.

Learn more about *The Mentally STRONG Method*: 1-800-55-STRONG ~ www.mentallystrong.com

Answer the following questions:

What did you decide to focus on and bring into consciousness during your meditation?

_____

_____

_____

_____

Were you able to identify your belief system? Who or what did you lift this to?

_____

_____

_____

What challenges if any did you face while listening for a response?

_____

_____

_____

What was the response and what choices can you make going forward taking this response into consideration?

_____

_____

_____

_____

_____

This is your Choice Opportunity to be Mentally STRONG® in active meditation.

Learn more about *The Mentally STRONG Method*: 1-800-55-STRONG ~ www.mentallystrong.com

Day 25 - Dr. B's Experience

Theme: Finding my voice and mantra.
Mood: Grateful, taking stock, and moving forward.

Today is Thanksgiving Day (November 24th), day 25 of my 45 days of grief. I had really hoped to be able to record everything, but this process has gotten exhausting. At this point, I think that it's more important to keep the process going (making sure that I'm meditating every day, trying to learn new things, and taking time for Controlled Grief). So, for the last couple of days, I haven't done a lot of recording, but I came out of the weekend thinking that I was going to accomplish a lot. If I'm not clear on exactly what I am doing, or don't have a solid agenda, I can get kind of depressed thinking that I am not doing what I am supposed to be doing.

It's still a lot of mental work, and I'm continuing to process everything. It's been very interesting that the learning and processing keeps moving forward. I did a brain spotting session over a week ago and I'm still working through what came up. It's almost like it's been unraveling in the background for all this time. I am still thinking about how when Johnny died, I lost my voice. It's particularly surprising because I love to talk. But I suppose that it's not really about talking. I feel like sometimes when I communicate my thoughts and feelings, the people I love don't get it or I feel stupid. Stupid isn't exactly the right word but it's what's coming to mind. When I was working through that this morning, I realized that sometimes when I say my *voice*, it's like I really want to scream. I want to scream for somebody to come rescue me. When Johnny was underwater and I was on that bank watching the divers try to rescue him, I lost my voice because I knew that he was already dead.

What do I feel like I cannot say? It really does come down to fear, which is a hard thing for me to swallow because I have an attitude that I'm not afraid of anything. But when push comes to shove, it is fear. It's fear of being wrong with my words, and of using my voice. I feel like I lied to Johnny, Cristina, and Kayla about being safe. I did not purposely lie, but it was still a lie. So, I became scared to be wrong. I've now learned through this process that there's no such thing as absolute rights and wrongs. It's more of a spectrum and a continuum rather than a seesaw. I like to process things externally with other people before I come to a conclusion. Once again, I'm still scared that I'm going to be wrong though. It also comes back to wanting to be rescued, but no one can rescue me. I have to rescue myself.

This fear of being wrong is a new concept for me. I am a risk taker and I like adventure. I would jump out of an airplane or dive off a cliff. It is very risky to publicly grieve and to make a documentary, but I'm doing it. It's risky to explore spiritual concepts that are outside of my culture, but here I am. It's risky to do a lot of things that I do, but I still do them. So, it is really hard for me to admit that fear is a part of this and that my fear has to do with being wrong. Maybe it's also a fear of not being liked. I do want people to like me, but I am also okay if they don't. There are other fears that are also strong for me: the fear of somebody getting hurt, the fear of something bad happening, and the fear that I will get hurt. I also worry about thinking that someone is trustworthy and then being wrong about that.

I believe that I can get my voice back now that I know that it really just boils down to a fear of being wrong. My voice has been muted since Johnny died. I tried to get it back over the 15 years following his death, but I kept getting proven wrong again and again. I would say things like, "Reggie's going to be okay," "God told me that Reggie was going to be healed," and then it wouldn't happen. Reggie would just be constantly sick. Every time I voiced something, and it turned out to be untrue, my voice became even more muted.

So much has happened to me in the past, but I am looking towards the future and my Personal Vision. Who do I want to be? What's important to me? I've been learning more about trauma, but I'm going to put that off a little bit longer. I want to focus mostly on grief during these 45 days. As part of that, I've been identifying my core connections, my triggers, and my expectations of myself and other people. Tackling that fear of being wrong is hard and can make looking at everything else even more difficult. I feel like God's telling me that there is no absolute right and wrong so *being wrong* shouldn't be my fear. I will work on that and on my new personal mantra, while trying to take care of myself and heal my body.

Because it's Thanksgiving, I really want to focus on gratitude today too. I am grateful for my story and my ability to empathize. I can use it to be a safe place to comfort people who have experienced injustice. Although I don't want to specifically fight for injustice, it's my choice. Instead, I want to be present for myself and others who have experienced it. I'm also grateful that I am working through my spiritual conflict. My eternal connection with Reggie and Miah is real, and I'm going to trust and utilize that. But there is more to that; I need to seek a relationship with God. He is even bigger.

Today's a travel day where I will go and do some Controlled Grief and movement. In Florida, I will spend time with family and friends (all of whom I am happy to have in my life). My sister is coming to help make sure that it is all documented (I have a heart full of gratitude for her!). And, as I've been journaling today, I've received many more answers, and I am also extremely thankful for that.

Dr. B's Controlled Grief and 5 SELF's Process Day 25

Controlled Grief: Arriving in Orlando was a Controlled Grief activity for me.

- o **Spiritual Self:** God is "bigger" than the "spiritual world." I need to try and connect directly with God (the source).
- o **Self-Improvement**: I read a book on intuition.
- o **Self-Movement:** It was a travel day for Thanksgiving. Travel is movement.
- o **Self-Regulation/Choose:** I mapped "Losing my voice." It boiled down to fear.
- o **Self-Care:** I have no expectations for myself on this travel day. I have been eating healthy foods.

My Controlled Grief Journey Day 25

Date: / /

What is your mood today?
(circle or fill in your own word)

Open	Loving	Sad	Guilty
Calm	Present	Depressed	Afraid
Relaxed	Safe	Broken Hearted	Overwhelmed
Hopeful	Angry	Irritable	Exhausted
Connected	Furious	Longing	Drained
Strong	Resentful	Disconnected	Numb

What activity did you choose to practice for **Controlled Grief**? _____

_____

What have you done today to empower your **Spiritual Self**? _____

_____

How did you practice **Self-Regulation** today? _____

_____

How were you able to work on **Self-Improvement** today? _____

_____

How were you able to prioritize your **Self-Care**? _____

_____

How were you able to work on **Self-Movement** today? _____

_____

Any other thoughts you want to remember about your **journey** today?

_____

Choice Opportunity of the day:

On Day 25, I traveled to Florida to do a weeping walk. I challenge you to similarly plan and schedule a weeping walk as well. This type of walk is about going to places where you know you will be triggered. I went to my children's school and other spots where they grew up. You should go to locations that are special to you/your grief experience. Participating in a weeping walk will allow you to release some of your grief.

Choice Opportunity: Weeping Walk

In this exercise you will plan a time for controlled grief. Plan for a day where you can travel to several places that were significant to your loved one. This activity will help you move the pain out of your body so you can cherish the relationship and embrace life.

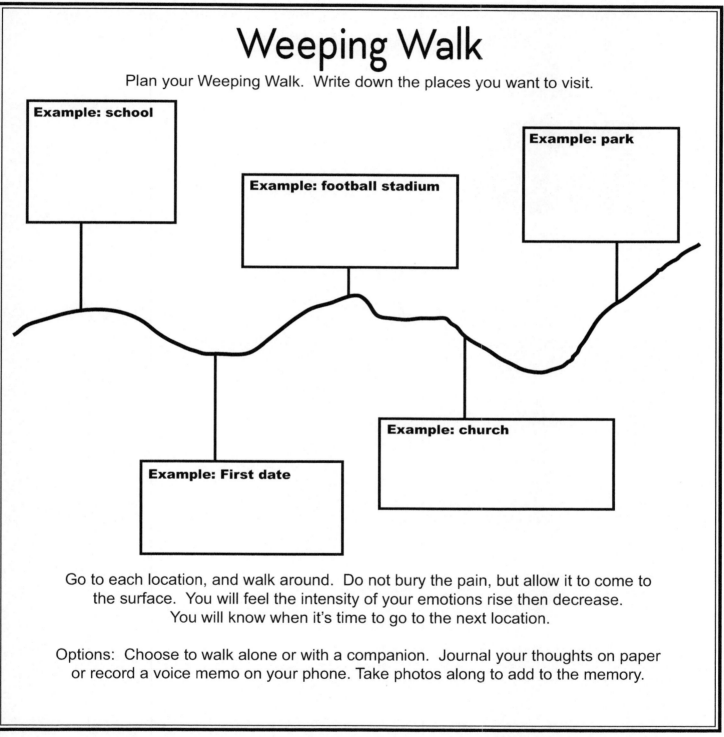

Weeping Walk

Plan your Weeping Walk. Write down the places you want to visit.

Example: school

Example: football stadium

Example: park

Example: First date

Example: church

Go to each location, and walk around. Do not bury the pain, but allow it to come to the surface. You will feel the intensity of your emotions rise then decrease.
You will know when it's time to go to the next location.

Options: Choose to walk alone or with a companion. Journal your thoughts on paper or record a voice memo on your phone. Take photos along to add to the memory.

This is your Choice Opportunity to be  Mentally STRONG®

Learn more about *The Mentally STRONG Method*: 1-800-55-STRONG ~ www.mentallystrong.com

*The Mentally STRONG Method with Choice Opportunities© Author: Cristi Bundukamara – not for reproduction/distribution

Journal

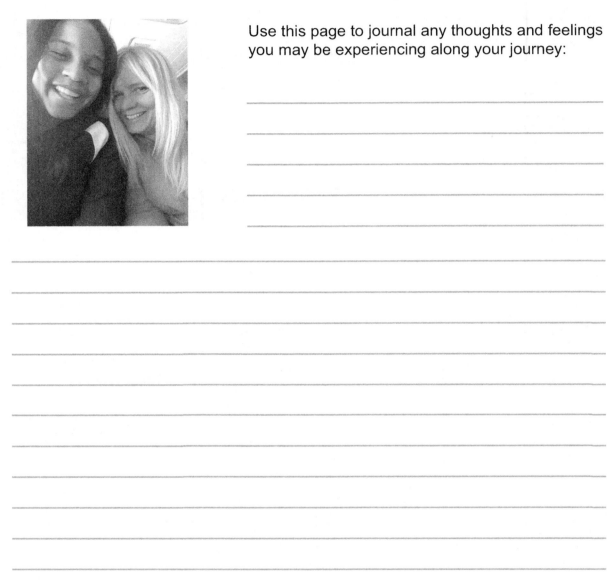

Use this page to journal any thoughts and feelings you may be experiencing along your journey:

_____

_____

_____

_____

_____

_____

_____

_____

_____

_____

_____

_____

_____

_____

_____

_____

_____

_____

_____

_____

_____

_____

Day 26 - Dr. B's Experience

Theme: Family connections.
Mood: Assessing and relating.

I am here in Florida and assessing the damage that the hurricane did to our condominium. It impacted the sea wall and the pool. Looking at the aftermath saddens me because it's another reminder that everything is always changing.

Reggie loved the beach, but Miah was indifferent about it. She liked the pool better because she loved to be around people, and this is where everyone gathered. The pool and the sea wall are just material things. The pool can get replaced, and the sea wall fixed, but the destruction is a reminder that nothing is permanent, nothing.

The ocean was very healing for Miah and now for me. But today it's cold and overcast, and the waves are rough. It's kind of like my life right now or my heart. I guess there's really nothing going on in my life that's so rough, but it's still the opposite of peace. I am in the process of cleansing, detoxing, and am supposed to be able to receive. I'm trying to talk to God, and just learning to meditate consistently and be aware. God is everywhere. God is everything.

As I concentrated on the cold water on my feet, the sand between my toes, and the back and forth of the waves, I thought more about God. What are you trying to tell me? I want to listen, but my heart is so broken now. The memories are flooding back. I have a video of Miah with a mermaid tail swimming in this pool that I cherish. I keep thinking about that. I want to separate the trauma from the grief and hold on to those endearing moments. I would not give that time back for anything.

Later in the day, I decided to take a walk with my mother on the beach. She was talking about how my father's death was my first experience with grief. I had previously mentioned to my mom that she never talked about my dad much and she told me that she felt bad about that. I'm not sure if her not talking about my father impacted me or not. I'm just processing some of the things that I went through as I'm learning about grief and attachment. My father was a big part of my life for the first 10 months, and then all of a sudden, he was not there anymore. Because I was so young, I didn't completely understand but I am sure that I still noticed it on some level.

I hoped to understand my mother's experience too, so I asked her, "What was it like to lose a husband?"

She said, "Well I immediately became a single mother and that sucked. But I had my parents to help."

"Otherwise, I would've been more messed up," I said.

"Exactly," my mother replied.

"It's kind of ironic that I will likely lose my husband too. I think I'm definitely at a more mature place than you were, but I still struggle a lot with anticipatory grief. I try to prepare for it emotionally and financially, but you never can really, truly prepare for losing somebody" I said.

"It made me feel bad because I was only, what, twenty? Right. I was twenty and I'd gone from daddy to husband and then husband to no longer husband. So, it was like I had all this freedom that I wasn't used to ever having to think about. Then I started partying a lot," my mother said.

"Did you ever actually go through a grieving process?" I asked.

"Well, I had snippets of grief, but no, I've never gone through a grieving process like you're going through," she replied.

"Yeah. Well, you've lost a lot too. You've lost a husband. And then losing your first two grandchildren. I mean, you were very close to Reggie and Miah," I said.

"I know. We lived next door their whole lives. No, I've never processed grief. I had a hard time with your grandma and granddaddy even though I anticipated those deaths for a long time. Then my dog Coco died and that was unbearable. I felt this intense pain here. I don't know if I've completely processed it all. I just know that I don't want a whole bunch more. Maybe I didn't process Reggie and Miah's death. So, I gave it all to my dog Coco," my mom said.

"That's what it sounds like," I replied.

"It's hard for me to share this stuff," my mom admitted.

"But I think, in our culture, we go through life not sharing it. You just talked about major grief in your life from losing your husband to losing both of your parents, to losing your first two grandchildren. After all that, your energy went to a dog. It's almost like that was a safe way to grieve, right?" I probed.

"Yeah. Well, because I've never done it," she responded.

"It's not a process that we've ever learned as people. Not intentional processing unless you go to a therapist or counselor. Did you ever go to a counselor, even when your husband died?" I asked her.

"I'm thinking. It was almost 50 years ago. No, I didn't go. I partied instead. I know that's disgusting," she said, embarrassed.

"No, it's not. Maybe you were ashamed. It's a reality of the fact that no one's ever taught us how to grieve or told us that it was okay. And so, it's one of the reasons I have this little rule of mine that I don't drink alone. Because I can see how easy it would be to have one glass of wine a night to relax and then it's two glasses and then it's, you're just using alcohol to cover it up."

There are quite a few people that have written books about grief. But back when this happened to you, it was like Elizabeth Kubler Ross was the one and only on grief, which isn't really that good. And those five steps, I mean, there's no order to them. But I do think you go through every step. Theories though are just theories. It's really more about taking the time that it takes. That's what I have been doing throughout this journey, and I am proud of myself for that," I said.

"I'm proud of you too," my mom replied warmly.

Dr. B's Controlled Grief and 5 SELF's Process Day 26

Controlled Grief: I took a walk on the beach with my mother. I also looked at pictures.

- o **Spiritual Self:** Nothing specific on this day.
- o **Self-Improvement:** I read *The Wisdom of Insecurity*.
- o **Self-Movement:** I spent time walking on the beach.
- o **Self-Regulation/Choose:** I practiced being present.
- o **Self-Care:** I spent time relaxing.

My Controlled Grief Journey Day 26 Date: / /

What is your mood today?
(circle or fill in your own word)

Open	Loving	Sad	Guilty
Calm	Present	Depressed	Afraid
Relaxed	Safe	Broken Hearted	Overwhelmed
Hopeful	Angry	Irritable	Exhausted
Connected	Furious	Longing	Drained
Strong	Resentful	Disconnected	Numb

What activity did you choose to practice for **Controlled Grief**? _____

_____

What have you done today to empower your **Spiritual Self**? _____

_____

How did you practice **Self-Regulation** today? _____

_____

How were you able to work on **Self-Improvement** today? _____

_____

How were you able to prioritize your **Self-Care**? _____

_____

How were you able to work on **Self-Movement** today? _____

_____

Any other thoughts you want to remember about your **journey** today?

_____

Choice Opportunity of the day:
Acknowledging your grief style is important because a balanced approach is a healthy approach. We can see differences sometimes, particularly in partners where one partner is emotional and connected, and the other partner has a more compartmentalized view. The best approach is a mix of the two throughout the Controlled Grief process.

Choice Opportunity: Acknowledge Your Grief Style

This Choice Opportunity is designed to help you identify your grieving style based on the Mentally STRONG Brain scale and help you decide how to use more balanced thinking around grief.

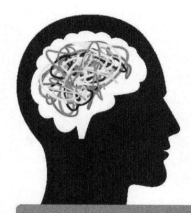  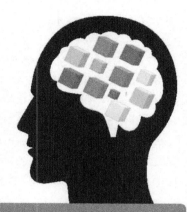

Disorganized Brain	Mentally STRONG Brain	Compartmentalized Brain
you can't control • A desire to always express outwardly • A need to connect every feeling	emotionally • Balanced reflection • Authentically exploring and processing thoughts and feelings	• Avoiding through problem solving

Similar to a Mentally STRONG brain; either extreme is unhealthy.

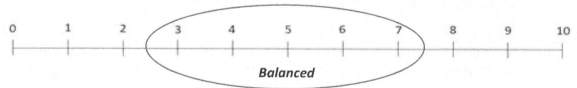

List in each box the different ways that you grieve:

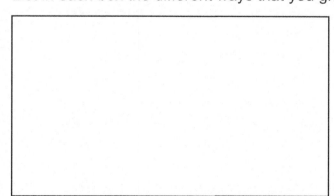 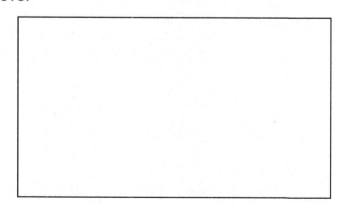

This is your Choice Opportunity to be _Mentally STRONG®_ in grief.

Learn more about *The Mentally STRONG Method*: 1-800-55-STRONG ~ www.mentallystrong.com

Day 27 – Dr. B's Experience

Theme: Bringing grief to the forefront.
Mood: Contemplative and supported.

I did some family grieving today which was a change of pace for me. We sat around and talked about our experiences. I recalled all of the old parenting books that I read in the past. It used to be that they said to let a baby cry in the crib until they eventually fell asleep. Reggie used to scream so much when I did that, and it became a battle of wills. Now, looking back, it's clear that what I read in the books was untrue. He had a neurological problem and that's why he was crying. Poor kid. I feel guilty about letting him cry it out now, but being a mother is never without guilt.

My dad told a story about Reggie when we were on our way to a dance party one day. Reggie wasn't quite walking yet but we picked him up and danced with him when we got there. We had a lot of fun and Reggie was laughing so much as we moved across the dance floor. His smile was enormous. What a great memory.

My family and I continued to share tales with the group. Each of my relatives talked about the last time that they saw Reggie and Miah and how much fun we had. Their birthdays and other holidays and events. We went through pictures together and felt both happy and sad. Life and death after all are both beautiful and bittersweet.

I think we unanimously agreed that when a baby is born, you never expect anything bad to happen to them. And when someone dies, it feels the same way. You're stunned and just trying to make sense of it. If you're able to communicate with a person after they've passed, that seems real to me. There's a cadence to life, and a firm beginning and ending feels false and unlikely. It seems more straightforward to assign life a meaning (vs. a beginning and an end). That meaning involves moving in and out of our world, and the soul's purpose, not a hard start and stop.

Our connection remains beyond death. As a mother, when you give birth to a child, you often have your child's cells left in your body, making you biologically still a part of them. It makes sense that you are, and that your souls are eternally connected.

I really believe that we've lost touch with the significance of death in modern times. My father talked about what it was like when he was growing up.

"It was a big deal when I was a kid in Kentucky. They had a death ritual that you went through every time. And it was pretty much the same for every death. They usually kept the body in the home, the living room typically, for a waiting period. People would stop by to visit the body and say their goodbyes. It was a little in your face, and their mourning was incredibly intense. I was really blown away by it when I was a kid, maybe even a little scared. But later I thought about it and decided that they got it all out right then and there. It was very intense yet just a normal part of our routine."

In our communities, we should be embracing death and grief much more than we are currently. To try to ignore the pain and just get back to "normal" as quickly as possible is only prolonging the anguish. Grief, life, and death should all be embraced in equal measure, notwithstanding the strong emphasis on our eternal connections.

Dr. B's Controlled Grief and 5 SELF's Process Day 27

Controlled Grief: I spent time with Grandma, Dad, and my brother talking about Reggie and Miah.

- o **Spiritual Self:** My stepmother saw Miah in the boat with us when my dad took us sailing in his boat he named "Miah."
- o **Self-Improvement:** I read *The Wisdom of Insecurity*.
- o **Self-Movement:** I spent time driving to locations for the purpose of grief.
- o **Self-Regulation/Choose:** Allowing myself to feel the pain of grief and allowing others to share their grief with me.
- o **Self-Care:** Family time was my self-care.

My Controlled Grief Journey Day 27

Date: / /

What is your mood today?
(circle or fill in your own word)

Open	Loving	Sad	Guilty
Calm	Present	Depressed	Afraid
Relaxed	Safe	Broken Hearted	Overwhelmed
Hopeful	Angry	Irritable	Exhausted
Connected	Furious	Longing	Drained
Strong	Resentful	Disconnected	Numb

What activity did you choose to practice for **Controlled Grief**? _____

_____

What have you done today to empower your **Spiritual Self**? _____

_____

How did you practice **Self-Regulation** today? _____

_____

How were you able to work on **Self-Improvement** today? _____

_____

How were you able to prioritize your **Self-Care**? _____

_____

How were you able to work on **Self-Movement** today? _____

_____

Any other thoughts you want to remember about your **journey** today?

_____

Choice Opportunity of the day:

For Day 27, I created this Choice Opportunity as I was sitting around with my family and sharing stories of my children growing up. I realized that although this is my intense grief (I lost children), my parents also lost grandchildren, and my sister lost a niece and nephews. We're all grieving. Bringing that different grief together is an important part of your healing.

Choice Opportunity: Grieving Together

Instructions: It is often hard to share your grief with others when you feel your loss and pain is more intense and so much different than theirs. I challenge you to sit and complete this worksheet with a friend or family member that is also grieving the loss of the same person. Each person will write how they are grieving on either side of the diagram and then come to an agreement on how they can or how they are grieving together in intersecting center. Although you may feel alone in your grief, this exercise can show you that connection can be found in grieving together.

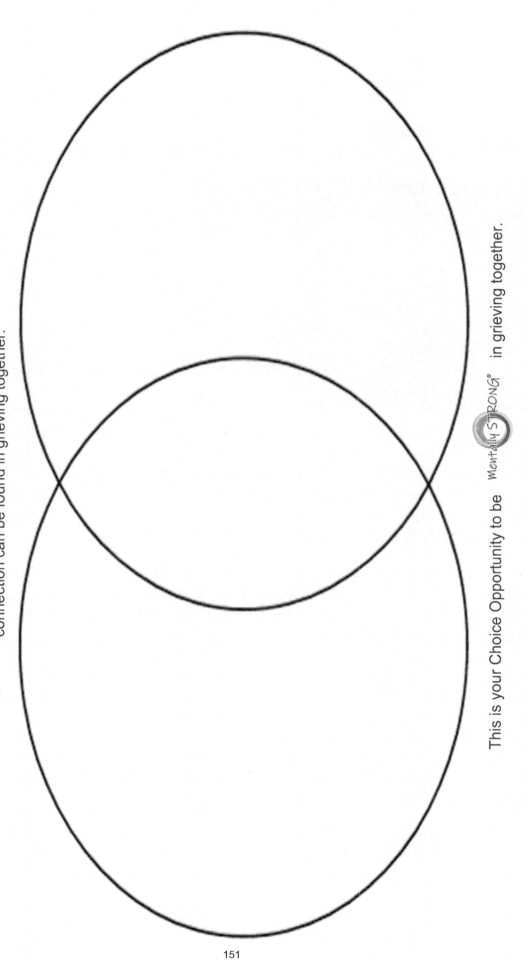

This is your Choice Opportunity to be *Mentally STRONG®* in grieving together.

Learn more about *The Mentally STRONG Method*: 1-800-55-STRONG ~ www.mentallystrong.com

Day 28 - Dr. B's Experience

Theme: Remembering and mending.
Mood: Relaxed and ready to let some things go.

I began the day by doing Controlled Grief, pulling out some old pictures of Reggie and Miah. They were in the backyard in Florida and looked so young to me, maybe 7 or 8.

Next, I drove to my old neighborhood, to see the house where I raised Reggie and Miah and the property where I grew up (the two houses are side by side). I've come to say goodbye to this property many times in the past, but I keep coming back. The memories and pull are strong. Bundy and I built this house ourselves from the ground up. It took two years. That was when I thought if I just did all the right things and took care of my family, that I could raise them in this perfect house. But nothing is perfect, and a house could not protect us from what was to come. It was a painful reminder but still the happy memories calmed me and made me smile.

Later, I did a Mentally STRONG Method session with Angie who lives in Florida. It was a massage and Mentally STRONG Method session rolled into one. I'm training Angie to be a Mentally STRONG Method ambassador, so it was the perfect combination of business and grieving for me.

I wasn't sure what to work on at first but then decided to map out the deep-rooted fear that I've recently identified. One of the things that I am afraid of is that I will end up having thyroid cancer because I neglected myself while taking care of others. I am also afraid of my mission which is to turn my pain into purpose. It's overwhelming and there's a large part of me that's afraid that it won't be well received. There could be a lot of judgement from my Christian friends, particularly related to the documentary that I'm creating.

It seems that my fear has shifted over time, it used to be mostly that I was afraid of death, specifically Reggie dying and then Miah. I've also been afraid of Bundy dying too. Now, I guess I have to add myself to the list if there is something really wrong with me. And, to some extent, I'm also afraid of Bundy living a long time to the point where he becomes an invalid. He doesn't want that, nor do I.

I can push aside my fears about cancer though. I don't really think I have it and if I do, thyroid cancer has a high remission rate. But then again, I tend to be overly optimistic. That is another fear that I am being too optimistic. I was that way with both Reggie and Miah, and then they died in the end. I've been holding on to all of this fear since Johnny drowned, and it's heavy. On some level, it has been impacting everything that I do.

Angie and I talked about where the pain and fear are located in my body. I feel like I've lost my voice (in some part) to this fear, and I also carry both the pain and the fear deep within my heart.

Angie said, "Let's try to open up the heart, and straighten it out a little so that the pieces can come back together. Think about releasing the damage and the cracks of your broken heart so that they can start to heal. Just kind of let them go. Imagine your heart just rolling out, even with the broken pieces, becoming flat so that we can see how to put it back together. Like a jigsaw puzzle when you turn over all the pieces. Try to just breathe and release it out. And then we'll work up through your throat, through your neck and try to release what's there so that when you get news tomorrow, whatever that news may be, there will be no fear. This is something that you can take care of."

I felt better after the session, as if I could receive the news about my health and embrace it, even if it were bad. I decided that I would also focus on mending my broken heart and getting my voice back to move forward with renewed vigor in this next season of my life.

Dr. B's Controlled Grief and 5 SELF's Process Day 28

Controlled Grief: I discussed with family that we're "never ready" for death.

- o **Spiritual Self:** I concentrated on the significance of animals in the fifth dimension.
- o **Self-Improvement:** I learned about dimensions. I also finished *The Wisdom of Insecurity*.
- o **Self-Movement:** I spent time driving to another location.
- o **Self-Regulation/Choose:** I made the decision to get an evaluation at a Thyroid Center.
- o **Self-Care:** I took a nap in the middle of the day.

My Controlled Grief Journey Day 28

Date: / /

What is your mood today?
(circle or fill in your own word)

Open	Loving	Sad	Guilty
Calm	Present	Depressed	Afraid
Relaxed	Safe	Broken Hearted	Overwhelmed
Hopeful	Angry	Irritable	Exhausted
Connected	Furious	Longing	Drained
Strong	Resentful	Disconnected	Numb

What activity did you choose to practice for **Controlled Grief**? _____

_____

What have you done today to empower your **Spiritual Self**? _____

_____

How did you practice **Self-Regulation** today? _____

_____

How were you able to work on **Self-Improvement** today? _____

_____

How were you able to prioritize your **Self-Care**? _____

_____

How were you able to work on **Self-Movement** today? _____

_____

Any other thoughts you want to remember about your **journey** today?

_____

Choice Opportunity of the day:

What should you do with your loved one's belongings? This Choice Opportunity is about helping you get through that. It probably seems very overwhelming but going through that process is actually a part of Controlled Grief. So maybe 6 months to a year after the person has died, go through their things. Put the items into three categories using the worksheet on the next page as a tool.

Choice Opportunity: Deciding What to Keep

When is the right time to go through your loved ones things and make choices about what to keep and what not to keep? This can be a hard decision for some, others may want to get rid of everything quickly. Challenge yourself to take the time to really go through everything. This is a type of controlled grief that happens over time.

Organise everything into three categories.

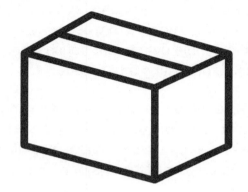

cherish

Take the "cherish" pile and decide how you plan to display or store the items.

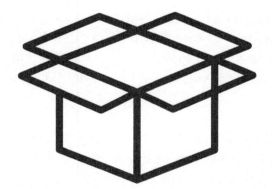

I don't know

Take the "I don't know" pile and pack it up. Then go through it again in one year.

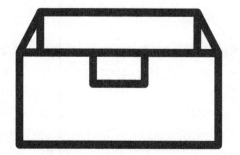

give away

Consider giving these items to those in need in honor of your loved one.

This is your Choice Opportunity to be Mentally STRONG®

Learn more about *The Mentally STRONG Method:* 1-800-55-STRONG ~ www.mentallystrong.com

Day 29 – Dr. B's Experience

Theme: Anger vs. cherished memories.
Mood: At home with the manatees.

I'm still in Florida. I got together with my friends Ruth and Stacy and reminisced about old times. We were talking about Reggie and how active he was. One time when we were passing out flyers in some random neighborhood for a Halloween Fest, Reggie just disappeared on us. We were frantically calling out to him when some stranger told us that he was just playing catch with the other boys. That Reggie! He was always playing and making friends. He would randomly bring people over to our house when he was young, even one time when we were in the middle of hosting a barbeque.

Reggie was my Rubber Band Man. He was able to bounce back from anything that life threw at him, until the one time when he didn't bounce back. Yet somehow, I had still expected him to. I think that there is a greater purpose in the pain of all of this. I have to believe that Reggie and Miah's lives were a large part of that major purpose. Johnny's too.

It was comforting to be with these two friends who had been by my side when it all started to unravel. They helped me and took care of me after I came back from Kentucky when Johnny died. They comforted me after Reggie's diagnosis. They just always believed in me. Even when I wanted to say, "F you, God, I can't do this," they were by my side.

Stacy told me, "God hasn't let you go. He hasn't stopped pursuing you. That's why I know He is real. He has somehow brought you peace in these storms. I've seen you struggle, but I've always seen you come back and be this steady, steady rock in your relationship with the Lord. It's been humbling to watch. It has. And I know that God is going to use you and your story."

I was touched by her words and, in my soul, knew that she was right. I've been learning a lot on this 45-day journey. You get to a point in your grieving where you have to acknowledge that you've actually worked through a lot of it. God has spoken to me throughout. Am I going to hold on to that anger? Because I can't keep going back and forth with it, and I don't want to hold on to it. So, I've decided to work on a statement of healing to integrate the anger at what has happened with the other things that I've cherished along the way. Even when we were going through difficult times here when Reggie and Miah were sick, it taught me (and many others) about life.

Stacy reminded me, "You let your kids live. You had parties for them and made everything a grand event. Most people would've sheltered their disabled kids, but you didn't. You let Miah have a boyfriend, and made sure that they always had fun, even with the suffering."

She was right. I did my best to give them as great of a life as I could, filled with all of the usual stuff. Later on, almost as a validation of that, I went to Reggie and Miah's old school. I spoke with the reverend there. When he pulled out some old yearbooks, I pointed out Reggie and Miah to him. He said, "I love it when people come back here. I always take them to the garden, it's the reason why I started one here at the school. I want people to remember that their family's roots are here. Everyone has roots, but eventually it's Jesus who waters them." I was warmed by his sentiment and the fact that he let me wander around.

I visited both of their classrooms but eventually gravitated towards the playground. They loved to swing, and I wanted to get some movement in for the day, so I sat on one of the very same swings that they had a long time ago. The memories came flooding back. They were memories of normalcy and contentment, or at least when I thought that things were normal. But what's so great about normal anyhow?

My sister, my niece and I went out for lunch at a little oceanside restaurant after we left the school. I was feeling pretty good about things, like I had given Reggie and Miah a happy life, at least as happy as I could. While we were there, the most incredible thing happened. We were sitting by the dock when a manatee swam up near the shore. She was jumping and playing! I think they were playing with Miah because she told me that she was there. The guy at the restaurant said that he had never seen manatees act like that, ha! He had never seen Miah before either. What an amazing moment!

The significance of that encounter was huge for me. Manatees are linked to mermaids and Miah always said that she was a mermaid. And on this day, she really was (and I got to see it)!

"Don't underestimate the power of your thoughts."
~ Dr. B

Use this page to journal any thoughts and feelings you may be experiencing along your journey:

_____

_____

_____

_____

_____

_____

_____

_____

_____

_____

_____

_____

_____

_____

_____

_____

_____

_____

Dr. B's Controlled Grief and 5 SELF's Process Day 29

Controlled Grief: I visited with friends and talked about Reggie and Miah.

- o **Spiritual Self:** Dancing with God.
- o **Self-Improvement:** I listened to *Becoming Supernatural*.
- o **Self-Movement:** I spend time traveling/literal movement.
- o **Self-Regulation/Choose:** I chose to sit in my truth, my present.
- o **Self-Care:** I've been cautious with my food intake and have been practicing healthy eating while traveling. I've been consuming the foods that I enjoy in moderation.

My Controlled Grief Journey Day 29   Date: /   /

What is your mood today?
(circle or fill in your own word)

Open	Loving	Sad	Guilty
Calm	Present	Depressed	Afraid
Relaxed	Safe	Broken Hearted	Overwhelmed
Hopeful	Angry	Irritable	Exhausted
Connected	Furious	Longing	Drained
Strong	Resentful	Disconnected	Numb

What activity did you choose to practice for **Controlled Grief**? _____

_____

What have you done today to empower your **Spiritual Self**? _____

_____

How did you practice **Self-Regulation** today? _____

_____

How were you able to work on **Self-Improvement** today? _____

_____

How were you able to prioritize your **Self-Care**? _____

_____

How were you able to work on **Self-Movement** today? _____

_____

Any other thoughts you want to remember about your **journey** today?

_____

Choice Opportunity of the day:

I chose the Choice Opportunity *Reconnecting After Loss* for you to complete today. It's often difficult to reconnect with friends or to make new friends after experiencing an intense loss. It feels like no one understands what you have gone through. This Choice Opportunity will help you work through and address those types of feelings.

Choice Opportunity: Reconnecting After Loss

Many times we withdraw from relationships after loss for various reasons. It is essential to realize that your relationship with your friends, family, partner, or spouse will be affected and thus change. Some changes may lead to a positive experience as these individuals may rally around you. Many times, it is not as positive. These changes, whether positive or negative, have a lot to do with the personal stressors that each individual experiences as they navigate the feelings that are common to the grief and loss process.

Why are you withdrawing from relationships? Check all that apply.

☐ The pain is too much.   ☐ I don't want to burden others.   ☐ It is awkward.

☐ I've changed.   ☐ No one understands.   ☐ I am offended by a comment.

☐ I am not feeling supported.   ☐ I value the loss more.   ☐ I'm angry.

☐ _____   ☐ _____

Who in your life do you need to reconnect?

What's holding you back? Could you extend some grace to them because they didn't know how to be helpful?

It is time to take action.

☐ Write a thank you note.   ☐ Reach out and call them.   ☐ Give them a compliment.

☐ Give a small appreciation gift.   ☐ Apologize for withdrawing.

☐ Communicate the reason maintaining the relationship has been hard.

This is your Choice Opportunity to be Mentally STRONG®

Day 30 – Dr. B's Experience

Theme: Letting go and learning to cherish.
Mood: On the road to healing.

I have learned so much about meditation and it's been very helpful. Because I'm an experiential learner, it's good for me to do an activity that helps me with my mind. I've been working on being present, like with meditation. I'm going to continue to meditate and receive until I love my life as it is today. You can imagine how difficult that can be if you have lost a child or a spouse or are dealing with intense grief. I'm learning how to separate myself from all of these things and just live.

One of the things that impacts me the most is my anger. I have a right to be angry. I have lost both of my biological children, and one of my adopted children. My family has been torn apart from all of this loss, and I feel like I have been left alone. So, I've earned the right to be angry, but it tears me apart from the inside out.

From now on, when I grieve, I want to cherish that grief. The act of ripping things sometimes brings me some release, kind of like with fire. I think it's beautiful, and I've liked using it as a symbol of releasing anger. When I'm hitting the punching bag, I'm getting it out physically, but sometimes I'm not ready to release it all right away. Anger can and should be released though even if it's only a little at a time.

My morning meditation has helped with that release. Meditation is about being present and acknowledging that there's so much more than what is right in front of me. I am proud of my past. As much as it hurts to have lost my children, I would not change a thing. I've felt some negative thoughts trying to take over, but that negativity is not my truth. Reggie taught me about life and being a fighter, and Miah taught me how to be content. I need to live in those lessons, standing firm. I don't have to fight, and I don't have to be afraid. Instead, I need to bring my energy up into my brain, and completely heal my thyroid, and all of my trauma so that I can cherish my time and leave my hands open to receive. There's something to doing movements that brings in positive energy, influence, and connections. Miah confirmed that I still have some things I must do to heal, and I am going to do so and make her proud.

Dr. B's Controlled Grief and 5 SELF's Process Day 30

Controlled Grief: Owning where I am in the process.

- o **Spiritual Self:** Dr. Dispenza's sitting meditation. Contracting three lower chakras to move energy to the brain.
- o **Self-Improvement**: I read *Becoming Supernatural*.
- o **Self-Movement:** It was a literal movement. I traveled back home.
- o **Self-Regulation/Choose:** I was triggered by my husband's anger when I walked in the door and responded back in anger. Then, I acknowledged that it was my present moment and responded appropriately.
- o **Self-Care:** I participated in HBOT.

My Controlled Grief Journey Day 30

Date: /   /

What is your mood today?
(circle or fill in your own word)

Open	Loving	Sad	Guilty
Calm	Present	Depressed	Afraid
Relaxed	Safe	Broken Hearted	Overwhelmed
Hopeful	Angry	Irritable	Exhausted
Connected	Furious	Longing	Drained
Strong	Resentful	Disconnected	Numb

What activity did you choose to practice for **Controlled Grief**? _____

_____

What have you done today to empower your **Spiritual Self**? _____

_____

How did you practice **Self-Regulation** today? _____

_____

How were you able to work on **Self-Improvement** today? _____

_____

How were you able to prioritize your **Self-Care**? _____

_____

How were you able to work on **Self-Movement** today? _____

_____

Any other thoughts you want to remember about your **journey** today?

_____

Choice Opportunity of the day:

For Day 30, I chose the Choice Opportunity *Choose Love*. It is about identifying injustice. Many times, when you've experienced intense grief, there is an injustice associated with it. This Choice Opportunity gives you the chance to determine what you can choose to do about that injustice (instead of allowing it to eat you up).

Choice Opportunity: Choose Love

Expected outcome: Understand how an injustice can impact your perception, your understanding, your behaviors, and your reactions. With insight and understanding, you will be able to understand and adapt to the injustice being experienced.

An injustice is a situation or influence that you think is unfair or based on judgement of factors that are illegal or outdated beliefs of others. Examples could be related to racism, gender, sexuality, political views, personal choices, group dynamics, social status, economic status, mental health status, homelessness, and so much more. Many times, the injustice is based in history and sometimes the injustice is a personal situation. You will have an opportunity to embrace the issue and choose to react with anger or love.

Instructions: Answer the questions below to explore the injustice root, affect, and meaning to you and your personal vision.

What is the injustice in your Thought Map? _____

_____

_____

1. Is there a historical similarity with your injustice? _____

   _____

   Is there a big picture within society, political, or personal trends? _____

   _____

How have others chosen to address injustice in the past? Usually those actions are based on a reaction founded in two emotions: Love or Anger.

2. What historical injustices are changed based on LOVE and which ones were changed based on ANGER?

LOVE   ANGER

3. How is the choice of LOVE or ANGER about the injustice impacting you from achieving your personal goals? _____

_____

_____

4. Choose to react to your injustice and list your reaction in the following areas. What are you planning to do to overcome the injustice?

LOVE

ANGER

5. What can you do to overcome the injustice? _____

_____

6. Do you need to forgive yourself? Others? or Both? _____

_____

7. Steps you can take now to continue towards your personal vision, after you had an opportunity to choose love. _____

_____

_____

Realize that you may not be able to change other people or the injustice. Know that you can overcome it with your choices about the situation or person.

This is your Choice Opportunity to be Mentally STRONG  and overcome!

Learn more about *The Mentally STRONG Method*: 1-800-55-STRONG ~ www.mentallystrong.com

Day 31 – Dr. B's Experience

Theme: Learning to cherish the good times.
Mood: Upbeat and hopeful.

Controlled Grief does not have to involve crying. During my session today, I listened to music, which was intended to make it more upbeat, but I still felt like I was going to cry. Yet, it was also a little turning point for me. I started looking through Miah's things. I'm not sure exactly what I was looking for, maybe just another memory that I could latch on to.

There is a lot of stuff here, toys and clothing, but also a lot of beautiful memories that I can cherish. My children really did have an amazing life and I did a lot for them. There's a painting of Reggie here that a woman painted because of the impact that he had on her. The three of them touched the lives of so many people and it was good to acknowledge and hold on to that.

I hummed as I rifled through all of the items. A song came on from 1970, one that my mom used to play for me when she was a single mother. She and I used to sing it together. We'd always loved it. Later, I sang it to Miah who loved it too. Listening to it now, it reminds me that I should be cherishing every moment that I had with Reggie, Miah, and Johnny.

I believe that Reggie's purpose was to bring me here, to this place, to stay with Miah. I felt Miah there with me as I sorted through the memories and invited her to dance with me. As I twirled around, I promised her that I would put my feet on the ground and stay solid. I know that the memories will get me through.

"I love you, Mommy."

"I love you too, baby."

I continued to sing aloud to her favorite part, more content than I had been in a while.

"Choose perseverance in your journey."
~ Dr. B

Use this page to journal any thoughts and feelings you may be experiencing along your journey:

_____

_____

_____

_____

_____

_____

_____

_____

_____

_____

_____

_____

_____

_____

_____

_____

_____

_____

_____

Dr. B's Controlled Grief and 5 SELF's Process Day 31

Controlled Grief: Dancing in Miah and Reggie's room. Me and You Against the World.

- o **Spiritual Self:** Nothing specific today.
- o **Self-Improvement:** Letting go of anger.
- o **Self-Movement:** I spent time dancing and walking.
- o **Self-Regulation/Choose**: Sitting in my truth, my present.
- o **Self-Care:** I participated in HBOT, visiting with friends, and haircare.

My Controlled Grief Journey Day 31

Date: ___ / ___ / ___

What is your mood today?
(circle or fill in your own word)

Open	Loving	Sad	Guilty
Calm	Present	Depressed	Afraid
Relaxed	Safe	Broken Hearted	Overwhelmed
Hopeful	Angry	Irritable	Exhausted
Connected	Furious	Longing	Drained
Strong	Resentful	Disconnected	Numb

What activity did you choose to practice for **Controlled Grief**? _____

_____

What have you done today to empower your **Spiritual Self**? _____

_____

How did you practice **Self-Regulation** today? _____

_____

How were you able to work on **Self-Improvement** today? _____

_____

How were you able to prioritize your **Self-Care**? _____

_____

How were you able to work on **Self-Movement** today? _____

_____

Any other thoughts you want to remember about your **journey** today?

_____

Choice Opportunity of the day:

On Day 31, you are two thirds of the way through your 45 days a grief. So, for this week's activity, it's time to begin to formulate a *Meaningful Relationship Statement*. For example, mine is something like, "My relationship with my children was very meaningful. I would not take that back even if I had known that my children were going to be sick. I would still want the time that I had with them. They taught me." This statement is not about your pain in grief. Instead, it is about the meaningfulness of your relationship(s).

Choice Opportunity: Statement of a Meaningful Relationship

Once you are at the point in your grief journey where you can acknowledge and process some of the pain and you have the mental energy to focus on cherishing the relationship, work on a meaningful relationship statement. This statement will describe what the relationship means to you and how they have positively impacted who you are. Here are some questions to get you started: What did they provide for you? What did they teach you? What is the favorite part of their personality? What did everyone love about them? How do you continue to see their energy in the world?

My Meaningful Relationship

This is your Choice Opportunity to be Mentally STRONG®

Day 32 – Dr. B's Experience

Theme: Realizations and owning my truth.
Mood: Taking action.

It's Day 32 and I am two thirds of the way through this process. At this point, I need to own my truth. Throughout this journey, I have been discovering what that truth is and who I really am. It's been coming together, and I feel like a lot of answers have been given. Now that I know, and have experienced it, it's time to own it. Once you've learned something, whether it's about yourself, your world, or your relationships, you are responsible for taking action! So today, I am choosing to act.

Yes, I've had bouts of anger come up for me during this journey. If you remember back on day seven, I talked about anger and how it's this protective layer. Anger doesn't completely go away after you deal with it, but when it comes back up, you're responsible for taking action. It's your choice! And on this journey, it's my choice. I choose to acknowledge that anger. I choose to be thankful. I choose to cherish my relationships with Reggie, Johnny, and Miah and to take the time to feel and remain connected to them.

Today was one of those transition days of just trying to put everything together. Looking back, I understand how important it is to stay focused on what you need for healing as you go through the consecutive days. When I did, things started to be revealed to me. For one, I realized that grief is in layers. So, I started peeling back the layers and working on all of the things that I found there. Now, I've realized that what I most need to do is to be able to identify who I am. I questioned what the truth was and then went through this process of finding it. The truth turned out to be that there are all of these layers. Now that I'm coming to the end stretch, I feel that I should shift and stay focused on what I need for healing. The layers of what is going on with me in my physical, mental, emotional, and spiritual health are all part of a lifetime journey.

I've been trying to embrace grief to make sure that I have effectively gone through the grieving process. Now, I've started to formulate a plan to move forward so that my intense grief doesn't negatively impact my future. Today involved a major shift in my thinking, a call to stay focused. What do I need to do to be able to feel like I can grieve and feel the pain, but also cherish my relationships at the same time? I can release the trauma. I know that now. It came up for me over and over again throughout. Self-care and sleep are two of the most important keys to healing and releasing trauma.

I will focus on them and continue the process. After all, the mentally strong journey lasts a lifetime.

Dr. B's Controlled Grief and 5 SELF's Process Day 32

Controlled Grief: It was a transition day where I took in all of the grief around me in my everyday life.

- o **Spiritual Self:** I evaluated my personal beliefs about life after death and the grief left behind.
- o **Self-Improvement:** I studied religions and grief.
- o **Self-Movement**: I walked on the treadmill.
- o **Self-Regulation/Choose:** Making the choice to refocus on grief with a plan for improving in other categories.
- o **Self-Care:** Gymnastics. I had a bad day at gymnastics. I couldn't get my body to do anything and was easily fatigued. I went home and got to bed early.

My Controlled Grief Journey Day 32

Date: / /

What is your mood today?
(circle or fill in your own word)

Open	Loving	Sad	Guilty
Calm	Present	Depressed	Afraid
Relaxed	Safe	Broken Hearted	Overwhelmed
Hopeful	Angry	Irritable	Exhausted
Connected	Furious	Longing	Drained
Strong	Resentful	Disconnected	Numb

What activity did you choose to practice for **Controlled Grief**? _____

_____

What have you done today to empower your **Spiritual Self**? _____

_____

How did you practice **Self-Regulation** today? _____

_____

How were you able to work on **Self-Improvement** today? _____

_____

How were you able to prioritize your **Self-Care**? _____

_____

How were you able to work on **Self-Movement** today? _____

_____

Any other thoughts you want to remember about your **journey** today?

_____

Choice Opportunity of the day:
Today is another day to embrace gratitude. This activity is about taking those things that you cherish about the relationship you're grieving and holding them close to your broken heart.

Choice Opportunity: Cherish Grief

Your heart may be broken, I challenge you to hold it together with cherished memories.

Write in your heart some of your favorite positive memories.

This is your Choice Opportunity to be  Mentally STRONG®

Learn more about *The Mentally STRONG Method*: 1-800-55-STRONG ~ www.mentallystrong.com

Day 33 – Dr. B's Experience

Theme: Miracles are overrated.
Mood: Disappointed and reflective.

As you follow me on this journey and live out your own grief journey, you'll realize that it feels like a roller coaster sometimes. I woke up on Day 33 disappointed and remained disappointed for most of the day even as I was trying to meditate and do my movement and Controlled Grief. Whatever I did, I was disappointed in the result. I want a miracle right now! I want this huge shift and I want to feel whole again. I want to feel the release of the pain. I want a breakthrough! But it's not coming quickly enough.

Because I was so disappointed all day, I decided to meditate on the concept of being disappointed. I was feeling let down because there has not been some miracle or crazy breakthrough yet in my grief journey. Upon reflection, I realized that looking for a miracle was also how I dealt with Reggie and Miah's DRPLA diagnosis and treatment. I was constantly searching for some sensational breakthrough treatment or something that would change the course of DRPLA in their lives. It didn't happen for me then and it hasn't happened for me now.

I lost a lot of hope when Reggie died. I thought I was doing the right thing with Miah because I shifted to thinking that time with her was a miracle. Yes, we still did treatments, but I wasn't chasing every little whim. Instead, I was spending quality time with her, but that time was cut short. She was not supposed to die!

Later on, I watched a Disney movie that I felt Reggie and Miah wanted me to watch (they loved Disney and animated movies). But again, I was still disappointed in it. I didn't get the message. So, I prayed and meditated about it. I asked why I was supposed to watch the movie because it didn't give me any insight or miracle breakthrough. The answer that I received is that I should live my current life and stay in the present moment, not get lost in a continued search for miracles. I guess miracles are overrated.

Dr. B's Controlled Grief and 5 SELF's Process Day 33

Controlled Grief: I watched the movie, *Soul*. I had a very physical reaction in the beginning of the movie. I had muscle spasms in my left leg, left side of back, and the left side of my neck. I was disappointed in the movie. I asked Miah why I was supposed to watch the movie, and she said, "Just relax and enjoy the movie, not everything is major learning." I realized later that the purpose was for me to live my current life.

- o **Spiritual Self:** Struggling with my faith in God and miracles.
- o **Self-Improvement:** I read Bonanon's *Trajectories of Grief*, Doke and Martin's *Grieving Styles* and K, S, N *Continuing Bonds*.
- o **Self-Movement:** I didn't do anything specific today.
- o **Self-Regulation/Choose:** Managing dialectical thinking that miracles are possible, even though I did not receive a miracle.
- o **Self-Care:** Nothing specific on this day.

My Controlled Grief Journey Day 33

Date: ___ / ___ / ___

What is your mood today?
(circle or fill in your own word)

Open	Loving	Sad	Guilty
Calm	Present	Depressed	Afraid
Relaxed	Safe	Broken Hearted	Overwhelmed
Hopeful	Angry	Irritable	Exhausted
Connected	Furious	Longing	Drained
Strong	Resentful	Disconnected	Numb

What activity did you choose to practice for **Controlled Grief**? _____

_____

What have you done today to empower your **Spiritual Self**? _____

_____

How did you practice **Self-Regulation** today? _____

_____

How were you able to work on **Self-Improvement** today? _____

_____

How were you able to prioritize your **Self-Care**? _____

_____

How were you able to work on **Self-Movement** today? _____

_____

Any other thoughts you want to remember about your **journey** today?

_____

Choice Opportunity of the day:

How do you make decisions moving forward? For today's activity, I want you to decide who you are and what you value so that you can make choices in line with those values moving forward.

Choice Opportunity: Let Values Be Your Guide

Values are what we cherish the most. They play a large role in the choices we make and the things we do. Values define what is important to us at our core. Understanding your values will help you recognize areas of your life that you have been neglecting or areas that need more attention. When trying to embrace life after a significant loss, you may notice that your values are in conflict. For example, a core value you may have is to cherish family time, but as a result of the significant loss you are avoiding family and isolating. Taking time to reflect on your values will help guide you back to a place of healing and recovery.

Check 10 values that are important to you.

☐ adventure	☐ equality	☐ humor	☐ order	☐ time
☐ ambition	☐ excellence	☐ inclusion	☐ parenting	☐ tradition
☐ being the best	☐ fairness	☐ independence	☐ patience	☐ travel
☐ belonging	☐ faith	☐ initiative	☐ peace	☐ trust
☐ career	☐ family	☐ integrity	☐ perseverance	☐ understanding
☐ commitment	☐ financial stability	☐ job security	☐ power	☐ uniqueness
☐ compassion	☐ forgiveness	☐ joy	☐ pride	☐ usefulness
☐ confidence	☐ freedom	☐ justice	☐ recognition	☐ vision
☐ connection	☐ friendship	☐ kindness	☐ reliability	☐ vulnerability
☐ contribution	☐ fun	☐ knowledge	☐ respect	☐ wealth
☐ cooperation	☐ generosity	☐ leadership	☐ responsibility	☐ well-being
☐ courage	☐ grace	☐ learning	☐ risk-taking	☐ wisdom
☐ creativity	☐ gratitude	☐ legacy	☐ safety	☐
☐ curiosity	☐ health	☐ love	☐ self-discipline	☐
☐ dignity	☐ honesty	☐ loyalty	☐ sportsmanship	☐
☐ diversity	☐ hope	☐ nature	☐ success	☐
☐ environment	☐ humility	☐ optimism	☐ teamwork	☐

Write down your top 3 values from your list of 10	Have your values been neglected or compromised after your loss?	Create a personal vision of the changes you can make to stay true to your values.
1		
2		
3		

Learn more about _The Mentally STRONG Method_: 1-800-55-STRONG ~ www.mentallystrong.com

*The Mentally STRONG Method with Choice Opportunities© Author: Cristi Bundukamara – not for reproduction/distribution

Journal

Use this page to journal any thoughts and feelings you may be experiencing along your journey:

_____

_____

_____

_____

_____

_____

_____

_____

_____

_____

_____

_____

_____

_____

_____

_____

_____

_____

_____

_____

_____

Day 34 – Dr. B's Experience

Theme: Controlled Grief is a life-long process.
Mood: Looking back and planning for the future.

As I'm coming into the final wrap-up of my 45 days of grief, I've realized that I need more time to grieve. Forty-five days just isn't enough. Part of these last 5 to 10 days is going to involve me creating a plan to continue in this grieving process. I feel very strongly that this is important. It won't be grieving every single day because that is too intense. I mean, I'm glad that I've been doing this every day but moving forward after I finish my initial 45 days of grief, it would be just too much to keep doing it daily.

Instead, I will likely be engaging in active grief weekly for the next 4 to 5 months and then choosing special days to practice Controlled Grief for the rest of my life. Probably the birthdays of my children and the anniversaries of their deaths will always be days that I engage in Controlled Grief. Those are intuitive and I want to honor them. I will also probably pick a few random days throughout the year. I suggest that you also take this day, Day 34, to plan your path forward with Controlled Grief after your initial journey. As you and I both know, Controlled Grief is not a one and done process. It is something that we should engage in for the rest of our lives.

Dr. B's Controlled Grief and 5 SELF's Process Day 34

Controlled Grief: I attended the Realm of Caring Holiday party.

- o **Spiritual Self:** Nothing specific on this day.
- o **Self-Improvement:** I studied psychedelics as treatment for intense grief.
- o **Self-Movement:** Today, it was moving around and talking with a family who also lost their child about grieving at the party.
- o **Self-Regulation/Choose**: I chose to be gentle with myself. The holiday party was harder than I thought. I chose to cherish the memories of my children.
- o **Self-Care:** No alarm. I slept in and went to bed early.

My Controlled Grief Journey Day 34

Date: / /

What is your mood today?
(circle or fill in your own word)

Open	Loving	Sad	Guilty
Calm	Present	Depressed	Afraid
Relaxed	Safe	Broken Hearted	Overwhelmed
Hopeful	Angry	Irritable	Exhausted
Connected	Furious	Longing	Drained
Strong	Resentful	Disconnected	Numb

What activity did you choose to practice for **Controlled Grief**? _____

_____

What have you done today to empower your **Spiritual Self**? _____

_____

How did you practice **Self-Regulation** today? _____

_____

How were you able to work on **Self-Improvement** today? _____

_____

How were you able to prioritize your **Self-Care**? _____

_____

How were you able to work on **Self-Movement** today? _____

_____

Any other thoughts you want to remember about your **journey** today?

_____

Choice Opportunity of the day:
When it feels like it's just too much and the grief and pain are so overwhelming, I encourage you to work through them and remember that you are strong. You've been through a lot but can still find joy. That's what this Choice Opportunity is about.

Choice Opportunity: When It's Just Too Much

Expected outcome: Learn to Identify and organize your stress and prioritize it to easier handle your overwhelming to do lists or decisions.

Step 1: STOP and BREATHE

Step 2: Give yourself some positive affirmations: _____

_____

_____

"You can do this!"

Step 3: Describe the things that are making you feel like it's too much, include everything:_____

_____

_____

_____

_____

_____

Step 4: What from the above, if it were by itself, you feel confident you could handle:

_____

_____

_____

_____

Step 5: What can you completely let go of? _____

_____

_____

_____

Learn more about *The Mentally STRONG Method*: 1-800-55-STRONG ~ www.mentallystrong.com

Step 6: An Organized Brain is a Mentally STRONG Brain! Break down the items into attainable tasks. This is the best way to reduce the feelings of overwhelm. Prioritize this list with the easiest items to address first and the most difficult last.

The "easiest" items. Complete and check as many of these off right away.

Some of these items may be more significant or have more weight. They may be time sensitive or have multiple steps. *Highlight or circle these.* These items may be toward the bottom of your list, however they will need to be addressed urgently when appropriate.

What I can fix	What I can't fix

This is your *Choice Opportunity* to be Mentally STRONG in overwhelm.

Learn more about *The Mentally STRONG Method*: 1-800-55-STRONG ~ www.mentallystrong.com

*The Mentally STRONG Method with Choice Opportunities© Author: Cristi Bundukamara – not for reproduction/distribution

Day 35 – Dr. B's Experience

Theme: Turning pain into purpose.
Mood: Connecting through shared experiences.

Last night, I went to a Christmas party that a lot of special needs children and their families were invited to. This is a community that we have been involved with in Colorado since moving here. Many of these same families relocated for similar reasons- to try to save their children with cannabis. Several of the children in this community have passed away, including mine. So, although it was a Christmas party, it was also a time of grief for those we've lost among us.

As part of the celebration, they called out the names of all of the children that have passed. I heard Reggie and Miah's names. It stung. But there was a family there that recently lost their daughter too who I connected with.

We sat and talked about grief and what we can do with it. I told them about my journey/process and how they were a part of my 45 days of Controlled Grief. It was good to discuss how we felt being there amongst all of the other children who were still alive. For me, that sometimes can be a trigger but overall, it was a comforting time where I could connect with old friends and people who knew Reggie and Miah.

Reflecting back on it today, I was reminded that I would be using my pain for purpose and that I will not allow myself to give up in this grieving and healing process. Neither will I allow myself to be depressed or have a life of pain. The pain that I have been through will be used for the greater good, and I will move forward.

Dr. B's Controlled Grief and 5 SELF's Process Day 35

Controlled Grief: I went through boxes of memories.

- **Spiritual Self:** Chakra meditation.
- **Self-Improvement:** I read a grief recovery book.
- **Self-Movement:** I walked on the treadmill.
- **Self-Regulation/Choose:** I used a thought map and map manifestation to understand my down feelings.
- **Self-Care:** I engaged in an acupuncture session.

My Controlled Grief Journey Day 35

Date: / /

What is your mood today?
(circle or fill in your own word)

Open	Loving	Sad	Guilty
Calm	Present	Depressed	Afraid
Relaxed	Safe	Broken Hearted	Overwhelmed
Hopeful	Angry	Irritable	Exhausted
Connected	Furious	Longing	Drained
Strong	Resentful	Disconnected	Numb

What activity did you choose to practice for **Controlled Grief**? _____

_____

What have you done today to empower your **Spiritual Self**? _____

_____

How did you practice **Self-Regulation** today? _____

_____

How were you able to work on **Self-Improvement** today? _____

_____

How were you able to prioritize your **Self-Care**? _____

_____

How were you able to work on **Self-Movement** today? _____

_____

Any other thoughts you want to remember about your **journey** today?

_____

Choice Opportunity of the day:
On Day 35, you should continue to find ways to honor your loved one. It's very important, but the methods to do so are not always obvious. My children had a rare neurodegenerative condition called DRPLA. Some people might think that I would want to honor them by giving money to research DRPLA, but honestly that is not where my heart is. I would rather honor them by telling their story. How would you like to honor your loved one? Determining that is what this activity is about.

Choice Opportunity: Honoring My Loved One

Intense feelings of grief may surface over and over again. Often times these feelings are triggered over a small personal reminder. You may feel emotions from sadness, anger, or even exhaustion. These feelings are a reflection of how important their life was to you. However, it is not healthy to stay stuck in your grief. It is important to stay constructive in your thoughts and choices. Set aside time to practice some "controlled grief" and honor your loved one.

Ideas to honor my special person.

- ☐ _____
- ☐ _____
- ☐ _____
- ☐ _____
- ☐ _____
- ☐ _____
- ☐ _____
- ☐ _____
- ☐ _____
- ☐ _____
- ☐ _____

Save this list and refer to it when you are down.

Honoring ideas:

- walk the dog
- eat ice cream or favorite snack
- visit the grave
- hold the ashes
- hold favorite stuffed animal
- listen to favorite music or song
- look through photo album
- cook their favorite meal
- watch their favorite movie

Take time for controlled grief, then return to your normal activities.

Suppressing grief for long periods of time is not effective or healthy.

Suppressing your grief until after work might be appropriate.

On special occasions or anniversary, take the whole day off.

This is your Choice Opportunity to be Mentally STRONG®

Learn more about *The Mentally STRONG Method*: 1-800-55-STRONG ~ www.mentallystrong.com

*The Mentally STRONG Method with Choice Opportunities© Author: Cristi Bundukamara – not for reproduction/distribution

"When my mind is my enemy, I will not surrender." ~ Dr. B

Journal

Use this page to journal any thoughts and feelings you may be experiencing along your journey:

_____

_____

_____

_____

_____

_____

_____

_____

_____

_____

_____

_____

_____

_____

_____

_____

_____

Theme: Attachment and eternal connections.
Mood: Understanding my grief.

As I've researched many grief theories throughout this process, there are two that stand out the most related to my experience. The first one is the attachment theory on grieving. For me, this is where my attachment to my children is the most intense physical, mental, and emotional bond that we can experience here on Earth. Studies have shown that this bond is chemical in nature and starts with the conception process. Growing a child is an energetic attachment inside of the body. Giving birth is next followed by creating oxytocin through breastfeeding. Then, being with these two individuals almost every day for their entire lives, that is the strongest attachment bond of all. Based on this theory, it makes sense why it hurts so bad and is so intense to lose a child. I'm not alone.

The second grief theory that I absolutely love is the continuing bonds theory which postulates that we are all eternally connected. I can hold on to that concept in this process of grieving but more importantly in the process of living and choosing to live moving forward. No matter what happens, continuing bonds will remain. I'll keep feeling my children's presence any time that I need it. And they will feel me too.

From all of the research that I've done on other people's grief work, those were the two that hit me the hardest and that I could most relate to. Maybe it will be the same for you. I encourage you to learn about grief as you go through this process. If you're curious, you can look at my YouTube videos where I explain these grief theories in greater detail.

Dr. B's Controlled Grief and 5 SELF's Process Day 36

Controlled Grief: I wrote a letter to Reggie.

- o **Spiritual Self:** Mapping manifestation. Walking manifestation.
- o **Self-Improvement:** I read Continuing Grief Recovery.
- o **Self-Movement:** I did gymnastics.
- o **Self-Regulation/Choose:** Choosing to apply my favorite grief theories to my healing.
- o **Self-Care:** I sat in the hot tub.

My Controlled Grief Journey Day 36

Date: / /

What is your mood today?
(circle or fill in your own word)

Open	Loving	Sad	Guilty
Calm	Present	Depressed	Afraid
Relaxed	Safe	Broken Hearted	Overwhelmed
Hopeful	Angry	Irritable	Exhausted
Connected	Furious	Longing	Drained
Strong	Resentful	Disconnected	Numb

What activity did you choose to practice for **Controlled Grief**? _____

_____

What have you done today to empower your **Spiritual Self**? _____

_____

How did you practice **Self-Regulation** today? _____

_____

How were you able to work on **Self-Improvement** today? _____

_____

How were you able to prioritize your **Self-Care**? _____

_____

How were you able to work on **Self-Movement** today? _____

_____

Any other thoughts you want to remember about your **journey** today?

_____

Choice Opportunity of the day:
Today, I want you to research a third grief theory. Read about it and then meditate on it. What did you learn from it and what can you use?

Choice Opportunity: Process using Grief Theories

 Use the Mentally STRONG Grief series or an internet search. Choose one or more grief theories. Study and/or meditate on the concepts of the grief theory.

Sample list of grief theories to get you started, various theorists:

- 5 Stages of Grief
- Dialectical Thinking in Grief
- Moving Through Grief
- Grow Around Your Grief
- 4 Tasks of Grief
- Physical Impact of Grief
- The 6 R's of Mourning

- The Dual Process Model of Grief
- Grief Work Theory
- The Grieving Brain
- Grief and Attachment
- Continuing Bonds
- Trajectories of Grief
- Find your own

In your own words, describe the grief theory that you chose:

_____

_____

_____

_____

Acknowledge any triggers or negative responses. For example, "that's not how I feel", "it's not that easy", or "I can never accept this".

_____

_____

_____

_____

Now reframe or minimize the above negative statements. For example: "Acceptance doesn't have to mean it's okay, it can be an acknowledgement of the pain, even if that pain is there for the rest of your life." Write your reframed positive statement below:

_____

_____

What did you learn from this grief theory?

_____

_____

_____

_____

Based on your personal grief journey, what criticisms do you have of this grief theory?

_____

_____

_____

_____

What is your personal take away from studying this grief theory? For example: coping strategies, interventions, change in mindset, or grace given to yourself.

_____

_____

_____

_____

This is your Choice Opportunity to be  Mentally STRONG® in learning about grief.

Learn more about *The Mentally STRONG Method*: 1-800-55-STRONG ~ www.mentallystrong.com

Day 37 – Dr. B's Experience

Theme: Understanding that relapse is normal.
Mood: Grief relapse.

I woke up sad this morning but still attempted to do my meditation and manifestation. As I walked on the treadmill, I tried to focus on having a good day, but I just didn't want to. I felt alone, alone in my pain and in the world.

My mind kept drifting because I'm afraid that I'll need to have surgery next week. I hear many people say that if you just think positively, you can manifest anything. Although I'm an optimistic person, it just feels like it's too much sometimes. I have trouble watching movies that are based on happy endings. Maybe it's because I'm still trying to find my own happy ending after losing my kids. There's a lot of pain today, so I'm going to feel it.

This was the start of a severe relapse for me. It all came crashing down and I wasn't able to accomplish anything. I was so depressed that all that I learned about myself in this process just didn't matter. I didn't care. I didn't want to do anything else. I didn't want to move. This has happened to me twice in this process. Once when I was going through the layers and talked about the fact that suicide was not an option for me and now today. I will never kill myself however that's the overwhelming type of pain that I felt today and on the other occasion.

I am disappointed in myself. I'm almost done with the process and here I am feeling like it's day one all over again. Like nothing matters and that all of this work has been for nothing. It's important that I admit to this brief relapse though because it's real. Grief work doesn't always happen in a straight line. Going backwards can and does happen. It's a genuine part of the journey.

When you have a relapse, call it what it is. A grief relapse occurs when everything seems as if it's all new and you haven't learned anything. But the difference is that you have learned so much. I have learned about myself on all of these days (even today) and acknowledging this relapse and working through it is part of that. It's actually made me stronger.

Journal

Use this page to journal any thoughts and feelings you may be experiencing along your journey:

"Unfortunately, you need to feel the pain of grief."
_~ Dr. B_

Dr. B's Controlled Grief and 5 SELF's Process Day 37

Controlled Grief: Lots of grief, but not controlled (grief relapse).

- o **Spiritual Self:** I struggled today and just allowed myself to have a grief relapse.
- o **Self-Improvement:** I had no energy to learn anything new.
- o **Self-Movement:** I walked on the treadmill, but it didn't seem to help. I was pretty irritable.
- o **Self-Regulation/Choose:** I chose grace for myself and being okay with a grief relapse day.
- o **Self-Care:** I did my HBOT.

My Controlled Grief Journey Day 37

Date: / /

What is your mood today?
(circle or fill in your own word)

Open	Loving	Sad	Guilty
Calm	Present	Depressed	Afraid
Relaxed	Safe	Broken Hearted	Overwhelmed
Hopeful	Angry	Irritable	Exhausted
Connected	Furious	Longing	Drained
Strong	Resentful	Disconnected	Numb

What activity did you choose to practice for **Controlled Grief**? _____

_____

What have you done today to empower your **Spiritual Self**? _____

_____

How did you practice **Self-Regulation** today? _____

_____

How were you able to work on **Self-Improvement** today? _____

_____

How were you able to prioritize your **Self-Care**? _____

_____

How were you able to work on **Self-Movement** today? _____

_____

Any other thoughts you want to remember about your **journey** today?

_____

Choice Opportunity of the day:

I created this Choice Opportunity after a grief relapse. What can you do to make sure that you are prepared for a grief relapse (because they happen)? Please understand that it's okay to relapse and have a day where you feel like nothing matters. Determining how you will pull yourself back up from that is what's important. That is what this Choice Opportunity is all about.

Choice Opportunity: Grief Relapse

As you move along your grief journey, you may have times where you feel like you are back at square one. All previous controlled grief seems meaningless, you feel down, maybe even depressed. I challenge you to make the following commitment to yourself.

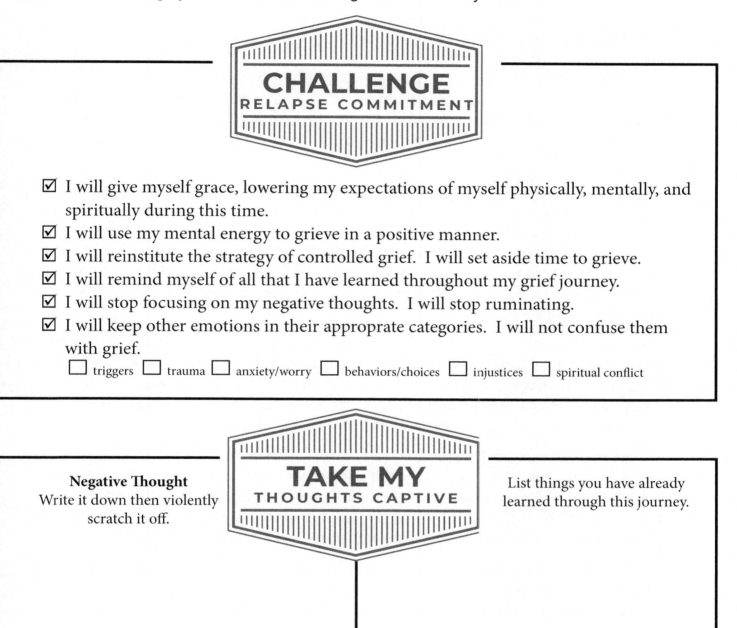

CHALLENGE
RELAPSE COMMITMENT

- ☑ I will give myself grace, lowering my expectations of myself physically, mentally, and spiritually during this time.
- ☑ I will use my mental energy to grieve in a positive manner.
- ☑ I will reinstitute the strategy of controlled grief. I will set aside time to grieve.
- ☑ I will remind myself of all that I have learned throughout my grief journey.
- ☑ I will stop focusing on my negative thoughts. I will stop ruminating.
- ☑ I will keep other emotions in their appropriate categories. I will not confuse them with grief.
    - ☐ triggers ☐ trauma ☐ anxiety/worry ☐ behaviors/choices ☐ injustices ☐ spiritual conflict

TAKE MY
THOUGHTS CAPTIVE

Negative Thought
Write it down then violently scratch it off.

List things you have already learned through this journey.

This is your Choice Opportunity to be Mentally STRONG®

Learn more about *The Mentally STRONG Method*: 1-800-55-STRONG ~ www.mentallystrong.com

*The Mentally STRONG Method with Choice Opportunities© Author: Cristi Bundukamara – not for reproduction/distribution

Day 38 – Dr. B's Experience

Theme: Processing my grief relapse.
Mood: Asking God for help and tapping into my inner resolve.

I am feeling really heavy today after my grief relapse yesterday. After all of this hard work, I just felt like I couldn't do it anymore. I didn't want to do it because I wanted something to change. Perhaps I still want someone to rescue me. Tonight, there was a full moon, so I lit a couple of candles. The red one was for Reggie, and the purple one was for Miah.

Even with the candles, I'm still sad. I've been going through a bunch of grief books, and just finished this meditation book. A lot of the teachings are about meditating so that you can manifest and get what you want in life. I tried but didn't get what I wanted so now I want to just learn how to be present. What is my current situation? That's what I hope to understand. Who am I without the kids? I've already worked through a lot of these things in my 45 days of grief, but this is a relapse. It all came back and it's hard.

Meditation is definitely something to maintain in your life for health, your physical health, your mental health, and your spiritual health. But it's not something that can be mastered. I am always trying to master and fix things, but you can't always do so. I couldn't fix my kids. I've been using cuss words against God today, and that is not okay. I really want to have a good relationship with Him and trust Him.

I am reading a book about a woman that lost her husband. I know that losing a spouse is hard. They keep referring to the book of Job in the Bible, as people often do with my story. God's not simple, He is not black and white. Nor is the Bible. Should we pray for miracles? They happen every day. I prayed for one and got nothing. It's not simple. I still believe though. I know that there is a God, a source, a something.

The book says that you take everything, but in my case, I feel like God took everything. Still, we are supposed to keep trying to find joy. I do try and my intentions are good. I feel like positive things should happen if you have good intentions, but it's so much mental energy.

I am angry and afraid, yet somehow still okay. During my meditation, I am trying to block out all of the distractions because I want to be able to concentrate and learn to love my life. I clutched Miah's rosary, the one that I had blessed for her protection (even though we aren't Catholic).

God, I need you to speak to me. Help me understand. Help me feel your love. God, hold me. I want to be rescued. Will anyone rescue me? It's almost like I'm calling on God to answer. He's supposed to be a rescuer. He's supposed to be a defender. I trust myself more than I trust Him though, and I don't trust myself very much. I couldn't save my kids. I need Him to heal my heart. One of my friends is going through this grief journey with me. She's going to set up a little alter tonight with a tribute to Reggie and Miah. I hope God sees that and helps me.

I guess I'm going to eventually have to read the details of Job. I'll just go to the final chapter for now:

> "Then Job replied to the Lord. I know that you can do all things. No purpose of yours can be. After Job had prayed for his friends, the Lord restored his fortunes and gave him twice as much as he'd had before. All his brothers and sisters and everyone who had known him before came and ate with him in his house. They comforted him and consoled him over all the trouble the Lord had brought on him and each one gave him a piece of silver and a gold ring. The Lord blessed the latter part of Job's life more than the former…. The first daughter he named, he had seven sons and three daughters."

I can't have any more kids, so my life is worse than Job's, I guess. I'm not entirely sure about it. I'm tired of being strong. I want to be able to tap into the strength and love of God like Job did. As I always say, when you're tired, go to bed. I probably need more sleep because I sure am tired. Sleep is so healing. I had an okay day today, but yesterday was bad. Today it's not as bad. I can do this. Like Job, I'm going to be okay.

Dr. B's Controlled Grief and 5 SELF's Process Day 38

Controlled Grief: Feeling the heaviness after my grief relapse.

- o **Spiritual Self:** I asked God for help and skimmed through the book of Job.
- o **Self-Improvement**: Reading *Grief Day by Day* by Jan Warner.
- o **Self-Movement:** Nothing specific today.
- o **Self-Regulation/Choose**: Managing dialectical thinking: God is good, but he took my children.
- o **Self-Care:** Making sleep a priority.

My Controlled Grief Journey Day 38

Date: / /

What is your mood today?
(circle or fill in your own word)

Open	Loving	Sad	Guilty
Calm	Present	Depressed	Afraid
Relaxed	Safe	Broken Hearted	Overwhelmed
Hopeful	Angry	Irritable	Exhausted
Connected	Furious	Longing	Drained
Strong	Resentful	Disconnected	Numb

What activity did you choose to practice for **Controlled Grief**? _____

_____

What have you done today to empower your **Spiritual Self**? _____

_____

How did you practice **Self-Regulation** today? _____

_____

How were you able to work on **Self-Improvement** today? _____

_____

How were you able to prioritize your **Self-Care**? _____

_____

How were you able to work on **Self-Movement** today? _____

_____

Any other thoughts you want to remember about your **journey** today?

_____

Choice Opportunity of the day:

After a grief relapse, how do you get moving again? Pain is inevitable but your response to it is a choice. You can continue to keep moving forward even after a relapse. This Choice Opportunity is about helping you develop a plan to do so.

"YOU WILL GO THROUGH PAIN IN YOUR LIFE BUT HOW YOU CHOOSE TO RESPOND TO IT IS YOUR CHOICE."

WHAT IS YOUR CHOICE?
WHERE DO YOU WANT TO BE?

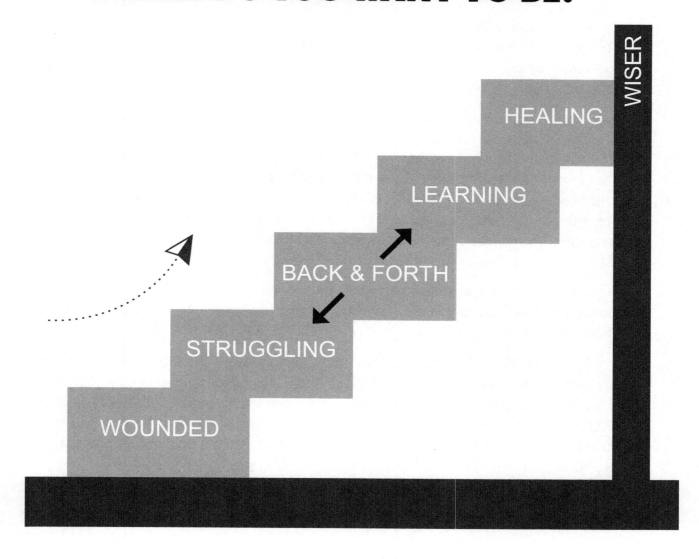

This is your Choice Opportunity to be  Mentally STRONG®

Learn more about *The Mentally STRONG Method*: 1-800-55-STRONG ~ www.mentallystrong.com

Day 39 – Dr. B's Experience

Theme: Continuing to process my relapse and moving out of grief.
Mood: Determined.

Many meditation gurus say that you should learn to harness the power of being alone. It just hurts so bad, being alone, but I can do it. I'm trying not to think about negative things, but there's also the everyday life stuff, the work stuff, the family stuff, the financial stuff. It doesn't stop. I want a break from these everyday stressors and hurts, but I don't get one. It makes everything that I'm thinking about worse. I can't fix it all.

I'm sad at how things turned out, so how am I supposed to be able to think positive thoughts and manifest positive things? I'm scared of making the wrong decision about removing my thyroid. And fear is not a vibration. Maybe if I were more spiritually connected, I could have changed the outcome of my kids, but probably not.

I try to stay conscious of my breath when I'm going down a negative loop like I have been for the past few days. I miss Reggie and Miah so much that it's confusing on how to take steps forward. Additionally, I've realized that I need more time, and that I still have some continued work to do. It will not be every day, but daily meditation is important so I will still do that. I will also focus on self-care and the continued bonds that I have with my children. I will love my life. I will show up for others. I will hold Reggie, Johnny, and Miah close in my heart, asking God to bring people to me that are part of the story and part of healing my heart and my soul.

I went to gymnastics today and it helped. Gymnastics is one of my favorite forms of movement. I've been doing it since I was a kid. It is a great way to push some of the grief out of my body. I am working on my back bend, back flip, and backward roll.

I think the Self-Improvement also helps me to remove the fear that's building up inside of me with this thyroid scare. I still don't think it's cancer. I feel like they're going to take out the nodule but say that it's benign. The nodule is probably a result of all of the trauma that I've been through, from the time Johnny died to the time Reggie had his first seizure right up until Miah's passing. So much fighting or flight and worrying about what's going to happen next. Who's going to get hurt next?

Reggie was in and out of the hospital his entire life, and it was very intense. Then, just when I thought I was getting over the grief of his death, I began to relax a little with Miah. She had seizures too, but they were well controlled. Even so, right when I started to relax, she died in her sleep. So, even when you think you can relax, you can't. Because of all of this, there's something emotionally stuck in my upper back, my neck, or both so I am gently working it out over time. My practice on my back flip is helping me with this too. My gymnastics coach told me today that she was proud of me for taking it all on! I will continue to make her (and my children) proud.

Dr. B's Controlled Grief and 5 SELF's Process Day 39

Controlled Grief: Sitting with the pain of grief and realizing how it has forever changed me.

- o **Spiritual Self:** I used tarot cards to connect spiritually.
- o **Self-Improvement:** I finished the book *Grief Day by Day*.
- o **Self-Movement:** I went to gymnastics where I worked out stuck energy in my upper back.
- o **Self-Regulation/Choose:** A friend hurt my feelings/energy. I used it to self-regulate.
- o **Self-Care:** I went out to dinner with friends.

My Controlled Grief Journey Day 39   Date: /   /

What is your mood today?
(circle or fill in your own word)

Open	Loving	Sad	Guilty
Calm	Present	Depressed	Afraid
Relaxed	Safe	Broken Hearted	Overwhelmed
Hopeful	Angry	Irritable	Exhausted
Connected	Furious	Longing	Drained
Strong	Resentful	Disconnected	Numb

What activity did you choose to practice for **Controlled Grief**? _____

_____

What have you done today to empower your **Spiritual Self**? _____

_____

How did you practice **Self-Regulation** today? _____

_____

How were you able to work on **Self-Improvement** today? _____

_____

How were you able to prioritize your **Self-Care**? _____

_____

How were you able to work on **Self-Movement** today? _____

_____

Any other thoughts you want to remember about your **journey** today?

_____

Choice Opportunity of the day:
In your struggle with grief, you learn so much about yourself yet there's still some back-and-forth. Despite that, you want to keep moving forward, learning and healing as you go. This Choice Opportunity is based on that concept and a theory that resonated with me. I don't feel like my grief will ever get smaller, but still know that I am able to get better (in terms of the pain) and can still find joy. Keep striving to get wiser and grow around your grief.

Choice Opportunity: Growing Around Grief

If you ever lost someone, you know that time doesn't make your grief disappear. Dr. Lois Tonkin developed the "Growing Around Grief" theory. She challenged the idea that time heals all wounds. Grief doesn't shrink with time but you learn to grow with it. The colorful circles represent joyful life experiences.

People think grief slowly gets smaller with time.

But the dark circle of grief doesn't change in size or disappear.

The reality is you start building new experiences around it.

The grief is still there, with life expanding around it.

How long has it been since your loss? Circle one

< 1 year

1-2 years

2-3 years

3-5 years

If you were to quantify where you are in grieving, how have you progressively created new joyful experiences around your grief?

Plan for embracing life: list things you would like to do to promote growing around your grief.

This is your Choice Opportunity to be Mentally STRONG®

Learn more about *The Mentally STRONG Method*: 1-800-55-STRONG ~ www.mentallystrong.com

*The Mentally STRONG Method with Choice Opportunities© Author: Cristi Bundukamara – not for reproduction/distribution

Day 40 – Dr. B's Experience

Theme: Pulling out of relapse.
Mood: Proud and looking ahead.

Day 40 was my Aha moment. I've been going through a relapse for the past 3 days but was able to pull myself out of it. I'm actually very proud of myself for that. The grief was overwhelmingly intense and felt like it did in the very beginning, like nothing mattered. When we're going through grief on our own and assessing our progress, we can feed off that negativity (that's what happened to me). If we stay there, it will turn into clinical depression or other things. Luckily, I was able to identify mine as a grief relapse. The darkness was only temporary. It is not who I am or who I will be. It is not a pain that I will carry into every aspect of my life. There is a sorrow that I will continue to carry but it doesn't have to affect me all the time.

On day 40, I can honestly say that I am almost done with these 45 days of grief. I pulled myself out of a grief relapse and have learned so much. Most importantly, I have figured out how to identify and deal with grief relapses because they will happen to me again. So, I will plan for that in the future and now know how to recover. Choosing to grieve and choosing to live are both choices that I have. I choose both.

Looking both backward and forward, I still feel good about the process of pulling it all together. I can now identify the different layers of my grief. I am beginning to be able to recognize who I am now and what my truth is. These last couple of days in my journey will be about speaking my truth. In the next 5 days, I will go into the 5 Self's again. I gave you a little brief about them in the beginning of this book and each day I've been challenging you on your 5 Self's: your Self-Care, your Self-Regulation, your Spiritual Self, Self-Movement, and your Self-Improvement.

During this journey is when all of it came to me- that your healing comes from taking those 5 Self's seriously as you move forward. Now, I want you to come up with a plan to move ahead in all of those areas. I am doing the same.

Dr. B's Controlled Grief and 5 SELF's Process Day 40

Controlled Grief: Sitting In my kids' room just letting it all sink in.

- o **Spiritual Self:** Meditation after Controlled Grief in my kids' room.
- o **Self-Improvement:** Considering my long-term plan for healthy grieving and how to communicate that to others.
- o **Self-Movement:** Walking on the treadmill while meditating, a kind of active meditation. Physical representation of moving forward.
- o **Self-Regulation/Choose:** Using the organizational skills learned in the Mentally STRONG Method to make decisions.
- o **Self-Care:** Mantra "I love myself unconditionally."

My Controlled Grief Journey Day 40

Date: __/__/__

What is your mood today?
(circle or fill in your own word)

Open	Loving	Sad	Guilty
Calm	Present	Depressed	Afraid
Relaxed	Safe	Broken Hearted	Overwhelmed
Hopeful	Angry	Irritable	Exhausted
Connected	Furious	Longing	Drained
Strong	Resentful	Disconnected	Numb

What activity did you choose to practice for **Controlled Grief**? _____

_____

What have you done today to empower your **Spiritual Self**? _____

_____

How did you practice **Self-Regulation** today? _____

_____

How were you able to work on **Self-Improvement** today? _____

_____

How were you able to prioritize your **Self-Care**? _____

_____

How were you able to work on **Self-Movement** today? _____

_____

Any other thoughts you want to remember about your **journey** today?

_____

Choice Opportunity of the day:

You can choose to have a good day and to find things to be excited about. This Choice Opportunity is about mapping manifestations. What do you want in your life? What do you love now? What do you love about things that you can see for yourself in the next 5 years? Mapping these things out now is important as you're almost done with your 45 days of Controlled Grief. It's been intense, but now is the time to start thinking about the future. I know that it's hard, but you can do it. You have a bright future.

Choice Opportunity: Mapping Manifestations

Unlike a Thought Map, in this exercise you are not going to be considering your past, writing anything negative or be pessimistic. Use the map below to map your manifestations using the following questions.

1) What do you love about yourself and your life right now?
2) What do you love about the next five years?
3) What do you love about who you are becoming?
4) What do you love about your spiritual identity?

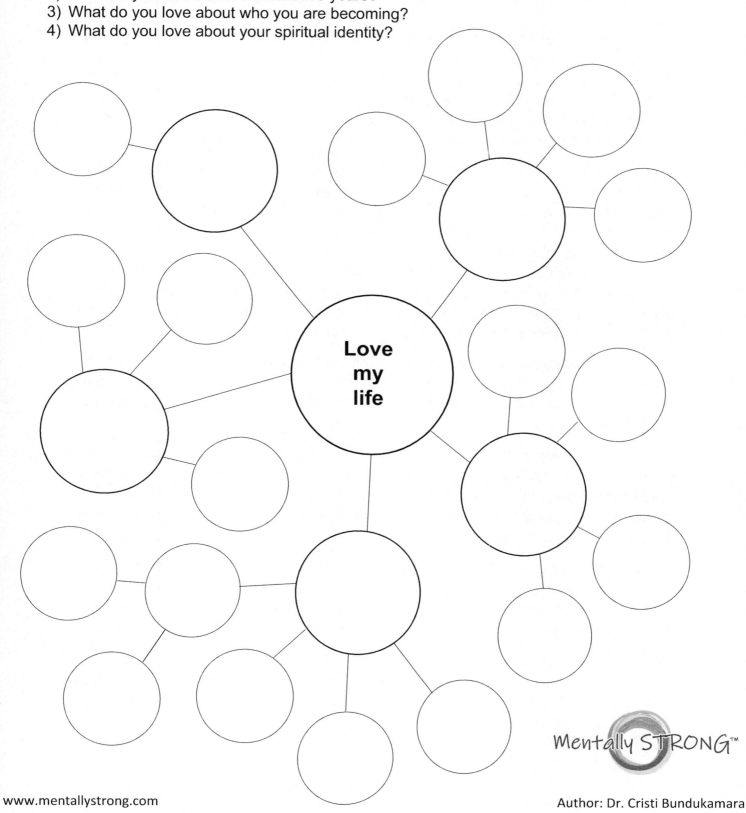

Love
my
life

Mentally STRONG™

Author: Dr. Cristi Bundukamara

Day 41 – Dr. B's Experience

Theme: Bringing it all together; the big picture of grief.
Mood: Embracing my spiritual self and looking back upon my progress.

I've been talking so much about what I've been feeling and going through during the last 40 days. Continuing on with my grief journey and these last 5 days, I want to share more about what I've learned about how we actually grieve. As you know, this whole process has involved me attending to my 5 Self's. Today, I want to focus on the first self, the Spiritual Self. Whether or not you are religious, it is important to take the time to evaluate your eternal belief system after you've experienced loss.

I participate in a Facebook group for grieving mothers. At least once a week, one of the members posts a comment on there that says something like, "Can somebody that doesn't believe in God please respond to me?" They get very angry and defensive because they don't have a spiritual connection. When people are finding their truth after tragic loss, they often turn to God (their truth), but that's not the same for everyone. You must think about your own spiritual health, it's tied to your healing. Even if you don't believe in God, you are still a spiritual being. We are all physical, mental, emotional, and spiritual beings. What does that mean to you? In terms of your spirituality, you must find that truth for yourself without someone else trying to tell you what it is.

In the Mentally STRONG Method, I have a category called spiritual conflict because it's so common. In the past, I let the church, pastors, and the people who had an authority in God tell me what my truth was. But throughout this whole journey, I've been working to find my own truth.

Another lady in my Facebook group posted that she saw a medium after she lost her child. It made her feel really happy and connected, but that feeling, and connection faded after about a year. The problem in that case was that the connection was between the medium and the child, not the mother and child because she didn't work to foster that spiritual connection.

As someone who has gone through grief, I know that you must find your own spiritual connection, or truth. There are two main types of spiritual belief systems. One involves God (or another higher power) pouring down their love. The other type, which most Eastern religions embrace, focuses on developing one's inner spiritual self through meditation.

Many people have what is known as church trauma or moral injury from people who claimed to be a representation of God. But in many religions, it starts with the self: self-love, meditation, and receiving. From there, it goes into universal energy. Notice that it doesn't stay with the self; it progresses. So, if you have any spiritual conflict, you have to deal with that first. Maybe you are angry at God like me, or perhaps you feel disconnected. Wherever you are, start by unpacking it further. For example, if you are adamant that there is no God, that's fine. Look into religions that are about self-love instead. From there, you will grow into loving others and putting that positive energy out into the universe.

After an intense loss, like losing a child or partner, you question everything, and you rightfully should. My truth might not be your truth; that's to be expected. The point is to deal with your own spiritual relationship. You have a choice. You can manage where you put your energy and how you react. Just make your spiritual self a priority, or it will hold you back in terms of processing your grief.

During my 45 days of grief, I attended to my Spiritual Self by engaging in meditation. There are many different types of meditation, but they are generally about resting the brain and receiving. Some of you might lean into prayer instead. Both practices are about developing your spiritual relationship (one that exists outside of yourself). Conduct some research to find your personal truth/spiritual connection and what that involves. We are all somewhere spiritually and should respect each other's progress and beliefs while moving forward to grow in this area.

Dr. B's Controlled Grief and 5 SELF's Process Day 41

Controlled Grief: I feel disconnected and afraid. I moved some more things in the kids' room.

- o **Spiritual Self:** Meditation.
- o **Self-Improvement:** Solidifying my grief process.
- o **Self-Movement:** I walked on the treadmill.
- o **Self-Regulation/Choose:** I focused on managing anxiety regarding reporting my medical status to the Navy and my upcoming surgery.
- o **Self-Care:** I went to a party at a friend's house.

My Controlled Grief Journey Day 41

Date: / /

What is your mood today?
(circle or fill in your own word)

Open	Loving	Sad	Guilty
Calm	Present	Depressed	Afraid
Relaxed	Safe	Broken Hearted	Overwhelmed
Hopeful	Angry	Irritable	Exhausted
Connected	Furious	Longing	Drained
Strong	Resentful	Disconnected	Numb

What activity did you choose to practice for **Controlled Grief**? _____

_____

What have you done today to empower your **Spiritual Self**? _____

_____

How did you practice **Self-Regulation** today? _____

_____

How were you able to work on **Self-Improvement** today? _____

_____

How were you able to prioritize your **Self-Care**? _____

_____

How were you able to work on **Self-Movement** today? _____

_____

Any other thoughts you want to remember about your **journey** today?

_____

Choice Opportunity of the day:
This Choice Opportunity is about your soul connection and spiritual self. Who are you down to your soul? Who are you to the universe/God?

Choice Opportunity: Soul Connection

Today the average life span is 27,412 days. Our days are filled with responsibilities and relationships. As we navigate through life we tend to care for our body and mind. However, we neglect the third part of our being and that is the soul. Our soul longs to be connected to something greater than ourselves. The soul searches for meaning and purpose.

Is there something more to life than what we can see and experience in the here and now?

What is my place in life?

Does my life matter?

Why am I here?

Who am I?

Suggestions to connect with your soul:

» <u>Daily meditation</u>: Download daily spiritual quotes, religious teachings, or the Bible. Reflect on the meaning.

» <u>Start talking</u>: Take time to clear the space and listen. Talk to God. Ask questions, search for understanding and wisdom.

» <u>Contemplate</u>: The human soul is the part of a person that is not physical. It is the part that lasts eternally after the body experiences death. What does life after death look like?

» <u>Write your eulogy</u>. What legacy do you want to leave behind?

How can you become more aware of your soul to fulfill what you are here for?

This is your Choice Opportunity to be  Mentally STRONG®

Learn more about *The Mentally STRONG Method*: 1-800-55-STRONG ~ www.mentallystrong.com

Day 42 – Dr. B's Experience

Theme: Using Self-Improvement to understand grief.
Mood: Leveraging remnants to understand individual experiences.

I am a self-improvement kind of person. I'm always looking for that next book or enrolling in some class. Because of my need to continuously improve, I knew that research and self-improvement were definitely going to be a part of this 45-day grieving process. That's why I made Self-Improvement one of the 5 Self's. I believe that we can improve ourselves by studying other people's work. But how do you use that to find your truth? It's challenging because many times we think that what we are studying or reading is the truth, but that is not always the case.

Most people are familiar with Elizabeth Kubler Ross's work related to the five stages of grief. It has been very well received, but how can everyone go through the same five stages in the same order? If you've lost someone, you probably want to say some cuss words about that. It just doesn't make sense.

Throughout this journey, I've read a number of books and studied several grief theories. Many of them had those same sorts of stages like Kubler Ross did. They talked about completing tasks and going through the entire process as the right way to grieve. Most experts claim that grieving is natural and involves a similar process for everyone, but when they compare the loss of a child to the loss of a pet, it can be hurtful. You are supposed to lose your grandparents, pets, and older people (as a part of life), but you are not supposed to lose a child. Still, we do grieve all losses, although the intensity of the loss varies and there is not one set, linear process as is suggested by many of the theories.

No matter what the process, we have to acknowledge that cherishing the person that we lost should be in its own category. As I went through the grief books, I found a lot of nuggets that were helpful for me although I didn't find any one theory that completely fit in its entirety. My challenge to you when you work on self-improvement through study is to not throw the baby out with the bathwater. You can always learn something from everyone (even if you are only using parts of what they say).

Take Sigmund Freud for example. He had a theory on grief called grief work. There are many things about his work that I don't think are applicable to mental health today. However, Freud studied human behavior his whole life, and there is good information that we can take away from that. My favorite Freudian theory isn't necessarily related to his grief work but instead involves the theory where he stated that depression is anger turned inward. That was a great notion for me because I've been dealing with so much anger related to my loss which has made me depressed. My Self-Improvement process led me to that realization, and to the fact that I need to release my anger. Thank you, Freud!

Many grief theorists put their life's work into these theories, and they believe them to be true. The majority of them use the word acceptance which is a complete trigger word for me. But through studying these theories, I was able to reframe the word. Acceptance doesn't have to mean that I accept what happened to me because I'm going to be wrestling with God over that every day until I meet him. I can't accept it, but I can accept the pain. I can accept the present moment too. I now know that I must embrace the pain in order to process the grief.

I talk about finding my truth, and you finding your truth. It doesn't just mean looking inside yourself, but there's some of that involved. There is also all of this collective knowledge that we can use to learn about ourselves through the process, but we don't have to take any of it as absolute truth. I realized for the first time in these 45 days of grief that I actually have trauma and that I am experiencing PTSD. I would not have acknowledged that before without doing some additional research. You'll likely be surprised by what you discover as well.

Overall, I had a very positive experience with Self-Improvement along this journey. I chose to dive into things that were very academic because I wanted to have that kind of base. Many grief experts tell you that as time goes on, the grief gets smaller and smaller. But if your loss is massive, the loss may never get smaller, but that doesn't mean that there is no longer any joy in your life.

Out of the many I read, I found the continuing bonds grief theory very useful, and I mentioned some of it previously. It talks about the fact that when we have a bond, there is an attachment which involves neurobiology and chemicals. Oxytocin is exchanged between a pregnant mother and a child, bonding them chemically. So, it makes sense that when you lose a child, that loss becomes catastrophic, and feels unbearable. The continuing bonds theory states that you do still have a bond there after death, but that it becomes a continuing bond through memories, memorabilia, meditation, communication, and knowing that your loved one is still present.

Now, you've heard about what I found on my journey, but on your own journey, you may find additional things that you can research for self-improvement and discovery. Lean into the process and use what you can.

Journal

Use this page to journal any thoughts and feelings you may be experiencing along your journey:

_____

_____

_____

_____

_____

_____

_____

_____

_____

_____

_____

_____

_____

_____

_____

_____

_____

_____

_____

_____

_____

Dr. B's Controlled Grief and 5 SELF's Process Day 42

Controlled Grief: I went to a Grief Ceremony.

- o **Spiritual Self:** I participated in a sound ceremony for grief.
- o **Self-Improvement:** I brainstormed about taking pieces from grief theories.
- o **Self-Movement:** I used sound vibrations.
- o **Self-Regulation/Choose:** Using knowledge to become self-aware.
- o **Self-Care:** I went to bed early for processing and preventing illness.

My Controlled Grief Journey Day 42

Date: / /

What is your mood today?
(circle or fill in your own word)

Open	Loving	Sad	Guilty
Calm	Present	Depressed	Afraid
Relaxed	Safe	Broken Hearted	Overwhelmed
Hopeful	Angry	Irritable	Exhausted
Connected	Furious	Longing	Drained
Strong	Resentful	Disconnected	Numb

What activity did you choose to practice for **Controlled Grief**? _____

_____

What have you done today to empower your **Spiritual Self**? _____

_____

How did you practice **Self-Regulation** today? _____

_____

How were you able to work on **Self-Improvement** today? _____

_____

How were you able to prioritize your **Self-Care**? _____

_____

How were you able to work on **Self-Movement** today? _____

_____

Any other thoughts you want to remember about your **journey** today?

_____

Choice Opportunity of the day:

I love this Choice Opportunity because we often go back-and-forth in our brains (head vs. heart). We say this and that and they often seem opposite. It's as if we're arguing with ourselves. Take a step back and ask what is my heart saying? How do I actually make a decision with my head?

Choice Opportunity: Logic vs. Emotion

Decision making can be filled with uncertainty and doubt. The decision making process can feel like a tug of war. This is because the two hemispheres of the brain think differently. Our brain is a bipolar organ. The left hemisphere reasons with your head. It utilizes logical and analytical thinking. The right hemisphere follows the heart and emotion. When making a decision, grapple with both sides of thought and narrow it down to the ultimate outcome.

What decision do you need to make?

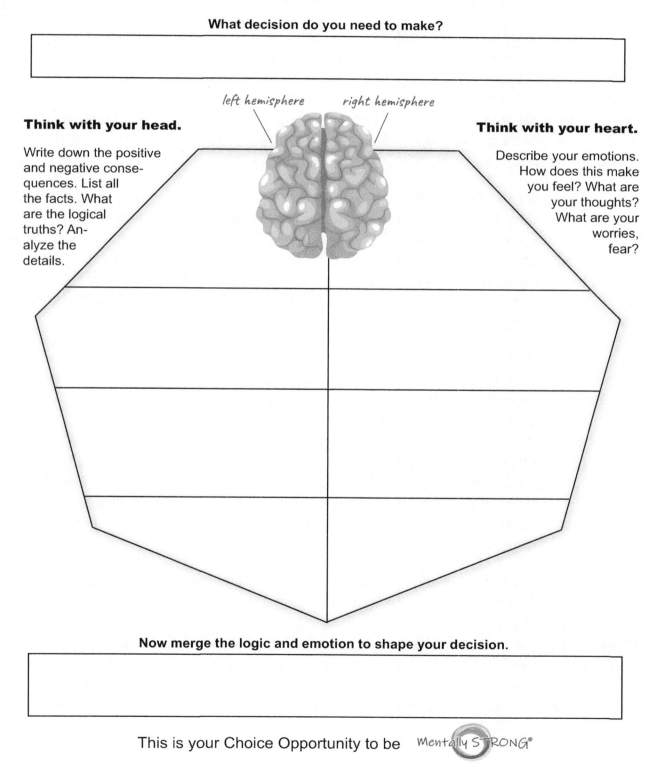

left hemisphere   right hemisphere

Think with your head.

Write down the positive and negative consequences. List all the facts. What are the logical truths? Analyze the details.

Think with your heart.

Describe your emotions. How does this make you feel? What are your thoughts? What are your worries, fear?

Now merge the logic and emotion to shape your decision.

This is your Choice Opportunity to be   Mentally STRONG®

Learn more about *The Mentally STRONG Method*: 1-800-55-STRONG ~ www.mentallystrong.com

Day 43 – Dr. B's Experience

Theme: Processing emotions through movement.
Mood: Finding and sticking with what works for me.

Today I want to talk about Self-Movement as a way to process grief and trauma. It's very helpful to move it out of the body. Our bodies are made up of energy, and emotions are energy. Eastern religion and medical practices often discuss the energies of the body. They treat ailments based on energy. We don't talk about that too much in Western medicine, but we do know that there is some truth to it. If we don't deal with things, there can be physical and emotional consequences for us. I've had physical symptoms related to my grief and many others have as well.

Emotions can get stuck in the body, but how do we move them out? We hear talk of releasing emotions, but in the case of intense loss, how does one do that? That's where Self-Movement comes into this process and why I included it as one of the 5 Self's. People who love to exercise will say something like running is my therapy. They tell you that if you go for a run, you'll feel better. Yes, that's working for them. That's their truth, but I hate running. It's not going to work for me. I'm just going to be pounding the negative further into my body.

Our bodies have a natural process for getting rid of things as we know from science. We take in food and toxins either by eating them or absorbing them through our skin on a regular basis. Our bodies learn how to metabolize those things and excrete them out of the body. If our body is restored to a positive balance, it can regenerate. Cells can also regenerate but it takes a long time. If you consume a toxin through your skin or ingest it, it might take seven years of healthy eating to metabolize and excrete it out of the body so that the cells will be able to regenerate. But it's all much more complicated than we might imagine and so is the process of moving emotions outside of the body. You are not going to be able to just go for one run and feel better for a long period of time.

The processing of emotions, just like toxins and nutrients, is natural and can be done on its own. But when the consumption of toxins (including stress) is higher than the consumption of positive things (nutrients, sleep, sunlight), then we start to have problems. If there are more toxins than positive things, how fast can our body metabolize and excrete them? Not fast enough. Our cells will not be able to regenerate, and disease will occur. The same is true of our emotional release outside of the body. We have constant input. Right now, you're dealing with some intense grief, and it feels like that's the only input, but you've had input your entire life (both positive and negative). If there's more negative than positive, like with extreme grief, then it's hard to keep up with the processing and releasing.

Nobody ever talks about how to process and move emotions. We discuss our emotions in general. Maybe we do so by talking to a friend, or a therapist (which is also movement). But what is not movement is rumination where you just sit in those negative emotions, wallowing in them, getting more and more negative. You're not trying to move that negative out and bring in positive when you do that. You must bring in positive when you want to move the negative out. So, the natural process should be that we have inputs of both positive and negative. We process the negative and release it, and that is where healing happens. But it's a long process. Intense grief and loss are like drinking poison and then trying to recover. It could take years. In fact, it will take years of actively trying to do it.

Movement is not just physical, but it can be physical. I don't like running, but I do like walking. I get on the treadmill and try to process and feel the pain to move it out. I set the intention that I'm not just walking for exercise, but that I'm trying to remove and release grief from my body.

Think about your life like a big ball you're trying to push forward. Sometimes you're moving along until you get to an obstacle. When that happens, you regroup and keep pushing the ball around it. Things in motion, stay in motion, but when something really powerful happens (like intense grief), the weight of the ball can become overwhelming. It's like you're trying to push it up a hill while going backwards. That's why we often experience depression and other physical and psychological symptoms with intense grief, and then we just kind of stop.

There are many people that I have talked to that tell me that they are dead emotionally and mentally since losing a child or someone close to them. I know that feeling. It often feels like I have nothing left. The ball keeps getting heavier and heavier, so I have to stop. I can't keep pushing. At that point, the goal is no longer to move the ball forward, but to just stabilize it and to stop it from moving backwards.

I know that the pain feels unbearable, but you can do it. You can move some of it outside of the body even if it's just a little bit at a time. It's not one walk, or one jog that will do it. It's the cumulative effect. Try to find different things. I've used tuning forks in my meditation, which is like sending a vibration. We can use music the same way too (as long as it's not depressing music). Whatever you do, make sure that it's something that you enjoy. I have found plenty of things that I like that move grief for me: a hot

Journal

Use this page to journal any thoughts and feelings you may be experiencing along your journey:

"Be comfortable in your story."
~ Dr. B

sauna, a jacuzzi, walking on the treadmill, or taking a dance, yoga, or gymnastics class. When I engage in these activities, I bring in positive energy and let go of self-doubt. It is a slow process but it's one that we must continue with to move our grief out.

Don't lock down and not do anything. Remember that it's about taking action, the action of movement. It can be gross movement, but some of it is also mental movement. That's why talking to a therapist that won't let you ruminate is also a type of movement. Additionally, as you recall, I went on a weeping walk. As you've read about, I took a pilgrimage to my kids' school and to dolphin therapy where they used to go. I walked around to those meaningful places and physically let some things go in the process.

Remember that processing through movement involves releasing a little bit at a time. It's not about letting go of the whole incident, it's about releasing some of the pain. That is what will provide healing, being committed to the entire process. If we don't release the pain, it will likely get stuck somewhere in our body and then mental, physical, and emotional symptoms could arise. If you've got any of these symptoms, take care of them (Self-Care). I believe in you and your ability to move. I believe that you are mentally strong.

Dr. B's Controlled Grief and 5 SELF's Process Day 43

Controlled Grief: As I listen to a grief book, I'm cherishing my children.

- o **Spiritual Self:** I'm intent on finishing my 45 days of grief and receiving insight.
- o **Self-Improvement:** I read *The Unspeakable Loss*.
- o **Self-Movement:** I traveled to Florida where my family can care for me.
- o **Self-Regulation/Choose:** Acknowledging only what is in front of me. Managing my anxiety/worry.
- o **Self-Care:** I went out to dinner with my mom.

My Controlled Grief Journey Day 43

Date: / /

What is your mood today?
(circle or fill in your own word)

Open	Loving	Sad	Guilty
Calm	Present	Depressed	Afraid
Relaxed	Safe	Broken Hearted	Overwhelmed
Hopeful	Angry	Irritable	Exhausted
Connected	Furious	Longing	Drained
Strong	Resentful	Disconnected	Numb

What activity did you choose to practice for **Controlled Grief**? _____

_____

What have you done today to empower your **Spiritual Self**? _____

_____

How did you practice **Self-Regulation** today? _____

_____

How were you able to work on **Self-Improvement** today? _____

_____

How were you able to prioritize your **Self-Care**? _____

_____

How were you able to work on **Self-Movement** today? _____

_____

Any other thoughts you want to remember about your **journey** today?

_____

Choice Opportunity of the day:
Today's Choice Opportunity is about self-movement and momentum as we push the pain and grief out of our bodies. You can do so through physical movement, spiritual movement, and other activities. What's in motion stays in motion, so this Choice Opportunity is all about making sure that you are moving forward with continued momentum. Your grief processing will be lifelong, but you are getting stronger every day.

Choice Opportunity: Emotional Momentum

An object in motion stays in motion unless acted upon by an opposite, opposing force. Does the concept "emotions are energy" make sense to you? Reflect on the storyboard below. Then, on the back of this sheet describe your experience as it relates to each picture.

"Life in Motion"

Everyone has a ball to push. The ball represents daily life tasks. These are the things that keep us moving forward in life.

"Opposing Force"

Sometimes emotional energy can be so intense that forward momentum stops. The task of pushing the ball becomes more daunting.

"Exert Force"

Forward motion will not begin until a force is exerted on the ball. This third step is the ultimate decision to make. Do you stay stagnate or do you exert a force to move the ball forward?

"Future Life"

Once the object starts moving the energy will begin to pick up momentum. As momentum increases, the force needed to push the ball will become less.

This is your Choice Opportunity to be  Mentally STRONG®

Learn more about *The Mentally STRONG Method*: 1-800-55-STRONG ~ www.mentallystrong.com

Choice Opportunity: Emotional Momentum

An object in motion stays in motion unless acted upon by an opposite, opposing force. Does the concept "emotions are energy" make sense to you? Reflect on the storyboard below and describe your experience as it relates to each picture.

Describe your life as it was moving forward.

1.

_____
_____
_____
_____

Describe the intense emotion which stopped your forward progress.

2.

_____
_____
_____
_____

What steps do you need to take to begin forward motion?

3.

_____
_____
_____
_____

Once forward motion begins can you envision a more positive future?

4.

_____
_____
_____
_____

This is your Choice Opportunity to be  Mentally STRONG®

Learn more about *The Mentally STRONG Method*: 1-800-55-STRONG ~ www.mentallystrong.com

*The Mentally STRONG Method with Choice Opportunities© Author: Cristi Bundukamara – not for reproduction/distribution

Theme: Self-Care as an aid to healing.
Mood: Active grief and Self-Care go hand in hand.

I'm going to talk specifically about Self-Care today (another of the 5 Self's). Let's start with the basics of self-car: food, water, sunlight, sleep, safety, and connection. I know that there are many people out there who have lost a child, friend, relative, or spouse, and have some sort of very intense grief. I also realize that they are probably not taking care of themselves the way that they should while they are grieving. I'm not talking about a certain diet or being super healthy. I am talking about the basics of just eating for fuel, staying hydrated, going outside, and finding sunlight, making sleep a priority, being safe, and maintaining connections. And, at some point in your life, creating new connections. Almost every grieving person that I talk to has some element there that is not being taken care of.

In our culture, we tend to speak about Self-Care in an almost indulgent way. It becomes about getting your nails done or having a massage. What is a one-hour massage going to do for you long term though? If you haven't slept in four months, what will a nail appointment do for your physical and mental health?

If you're not eating right, or drinking enough water, connections become super important. Sadly, however, they are often the first thing that we push away from. It's logical. Nobody understands our pain. Although that may be true, it doesn't mean that we don't need other people or that they don't want to help. Someone doesn't need to understand your pain to be empathetic to your situation.

When you think about the basics that I mentioned, ask yourself which of those things you're ignoring or neglecting. Do some self-evaluation here. What do you need to start taking better care of? Do you have something that's counteracting that? Are you drinking too much? Are you using substances that bring you down? This is an important aspect of self-care. One of the rules that I made for myself involves guidelines around indulging in substances. I have a very strong addiction history on my biological father's side of the family. I also scored high on addiction scales back when I was trying to be a missionary. So, I have concluded that I likely have an addictive personality and can see how easy it would be to overindulge.

If you've lost your child or spouse, you might start with one glass of wine to wind down and get to sleep, but then it's two glasses of wine, and then a year later, it's a whole bottle. Because of that possibility, I gave myself a solid rule as I mentioned earlier

"Happiness is a series of moments, choose your happy moments."
~ Dr. B

Use this page to journal any thoughts and feelings you may be experiencing along your journey:

_____

_____

_____

_____

_____

_____

_____

_____

_____

_____

_____

_____

_____

_____

_____

_____

_____

_____

_____

in this book. I will never drink alcohol when I'm alone. I'm not telling you what you should and shouldn't do. Just always ask yourself if you're doing something that might make it worse. Or are you doing something to hurt yourself? In an extreme case, which could be suicidal ideations or cutting which are obviously the opposite of self-care. If stopping any of these harmful things feels impossible to do, then seek professional help.

I've been working on myself from a mental health/psychological standpoint for many years, and the death of my children was still unbearable and difficult. So, wherever you are on your journey, it's your journey. I can tell you for myself, even though I'm a go-getter Type A personality and I'm healthy, I have been experiencing cognitive symptoms since 2016. My test scores showed difficulty concentrating and inattention. Then, after Miah's death, the cognitive symptoms became worse. I was really having trouble pulling it together. My memory and attention to detail were quite impaired. That's when I went for the brain scan and follow up which led to a deeper dive into my health (as an extended form of Self-Care). I've been having medical tests throughout my 45 days of grief and have uncovered some minor health issues that I am addressing.

It all starts with the basics though. Getting sleep is so hard after trauma and intense grief. My daughter died in the middle of the night when I was sound asleep. So, I often wake up in a panic, and as you can imagine, making sleep a priority can be difficult. But it's okay to find that balance, and that is what I am working towards every day.

What is your self-care? Define it and commit to improving it throughout this journey and beyond!

Dr. B's Controlled Grief and 5 SELF's Process Day 44

Controlled Grief: Thinking about how hard it was to take care of myself when my children were alive.

- o **Spiritual Self:** I meditated before going under anesthesia. I asked God to give me a spiritual experience but woke up with nothing.
- o **Self-Improvement:** Nothing specific on this day. I am continuing to improve.
- o **Self-Movement:** Removing the thyroid was like a physical manifestation of removing the trauma from my life.
- o **Self-Regulation/Choose:** I regulated my emotions around caring for myself. Choosing to have my thyroid removed.
- o **Self-Care:** Just do it, and don't second guess yourself.

My Controlled Grief Journey Day 44

Date: /   /

What is your mood today?
(circle or fill in your own word)

Open	Loving	Sad	Guilty
Calm	Present	Depressed	Afraid
Relaxed	Safe	Broken Hearted	Overwhelmed
Hopeful	Angry	Irritable	Exhausted
Connected	Furious	Longing	Drained
Strong	Resentful	Disconnected	Numb

What activity did you choose to practice for **Controlled Grief**? _____

_____

What have you done today to empower your **Spiritual Self**? _____

_____

How did you practice **Self-Regulation** today? _____

_____

How were you able to work on **Self-Improvement** today? _____

_____

How were you able to prioritize your **Self-Care**? _____

_____

How were you able to work on **Self-Movement** today? _____

_____

Any other thoughts you want to remember about your **journey** today?

_____

Choice Opportunity of the day:
This Choice Opportunity is about making sure that you are taking time to care for yourself. It goes back to eating healthy foods, drinking plenty of water, and getting enough sleep but it is also about finding and doing things that you enjoy. What fills your cup?

What does self-care mean to you?

We often attempt to make time for self-care, but we don't feel refreshed. What do you think contributes to not feeling refreshed after self-care activities?

_____

_____

_____

Think about your own self-care. What activity truely gives you something that "fills your cup". Think of an activity that gives you energy but doesn't zap your energy. This will be different for everyone. Take the time to understand yourself and choose activities that "fill your cup". That is self-care.

ONE TIME LOVE IT ACTIVITY	ACTIVITY TO ADD TO DAILY ROUTINE	LONG TERM SELF-CARE GOAL

This is your Choice Opportunity to be Mentally STRONG®

Learn more about *The Mentally STRONG Method*: **1-800-55-STRONG ~ www.mentallystrong.com**

*The Mentally STRONG Method with Choice Opportunities© Author: Cristi Bundukamara – not for reproduction/distribution

Day 45 – Dr. B's Experience

Theme: Self-Regulation is the key to recovery.
Mood: Bittersweet and resolute.

As I complete the 45ᵗʰ day, on the anniversary of Miah's death, it's bittersweet. I am sad, yet triumphant because I have done what I set out to do. It's been challenging, but I made it. A lot of that had to do with my ability to self-regulate and go on with my day after engaging in active grief. That's why Self-Regulation is the last of the 5 Self's in this process. You might not have control over what/who you lost, but you are always in control over yourself.

I know that it can be taxing, and maybe you feel like you can't self-regulate. I can understand that. Something happened to you that was not your fault. We have this false sense that we're in control of everything in our lives. Unfortunately, that's not true. We are really only in control of two things: how and where we spend our energy, and how we react to what is happening.

You are processing intense grief right now, but you do have control. It's hard for many of my patients to understand that. We often take the victim stance. I've done it before. It's easy to fall into a negative spiral, but you can control where you spend your energy. It's about trying to reframe things and working to focus on the positive. Think about what you are grateful for and how/where you can find joy. Grief is so intense that you must work hard to find those positives because the pain of the negatives is so heavy. But, again, you have control in terms of how you respond and react to the things that happen to you.

There's no such thing as a pain-free life. Everyone experiences pain. Some more than others, and I've had more of it than many. I lost Johnny in the drowning accident. Then, I got this terminal diagnosis for Reggie and Miah as well as my husband. The whole time, I kept thinking that nothing else could happen. Surely if there is a God, He would protect my children. But they were not protected, and He took them away.

All sorts of emotions can get intertwined while doing Controlled Grief. Grief is about feeling the pain of loss, but we must find a way to pull ourselves out of it and return to our lives. That's where Self-Regulation comes in. The Mentally Strong Method involves thinking, organizing, and choosing. You must think through your problems and look at your present situation as well as your past- including insecurities and negative beliefs about your environment (they are impacting your grief).

One of the negative thoughts that I often have is: why is everything so hard? That's a core connection. It probably started in my childhood when I had trouble with academics. Core connections don't really have to do with grief, but when I'm upset and not self-regulating, they resurface. Many people want to control their triggers by trying to avoid certain things. Avoiding them is not always practical though. We have the ability to self-regulate in response to our triggers, and sometimes that means communicating boundaries, but not always.

A trigger pushes a core connection button. You can't just positively self-talk your way out of grief, trauma, or being a victim of trauma. I would probably say a hundred percent of the people who have lost a child or someone dear to them are going to have a trauma response. Losing a child is probably one of the worst things that could ever happen to somebody. It took me going through this 45-days of grief and seeing my brain scan to realize that I had been dealing with so much trauma. My son Reggie was hospitalized at least twenty times. His femur broke in front of me during a seizure. I found my daughter dead. I watched the divers look for and pull Johnny's lifeless body from the water. That's trauma, but it gets enmeshed with grief. And so, we have to separate those things.

I'll admit that it's a lot of negativities to surround yourself with. I bet every single one of you is doubting yourself or talking negatively about yourself. For me, I have those sort of linking thoughts like I didn't do enough, I'm not a good mother, I didn't spend enough time, and I should have slept with Miah that night. That's why it can feel unrealistic to think positively. How can I think positively after all of that? Well, the only thing that is going to help you is to deal with your trauma and stop talking to yourself negatively. That's what I've been teaching myself to do.

So, what are you doing to help yourself? You might have anxiety, but you can self-regulate it. Maybe you can't make it go away completely, but you can manage it. Perhaps you are dealing with injustice. Many people believe that the death of their child or their spouse was a major injustice, in the case of a DUI or murder for example. That injustice also gets tangled up in your grief. We want to feel the pain and cherish the relationship so that we can find our truth, our purpose, and not get stuck in those injustices. Spiritual conflict falls in there too. You must address your spiritual health and any spiritual conflicts that are lingering. And then lastly is the addiction category. This can be drug addiction or being addicted to negative thoughts/rumination.

You have earned the right to feel depressed, but don't become addicted to a negative process. Can you stop it? Yes! I feel like my purpose and my passion is to empower people to do so. But many times, that first choice is getting professional help. Self-regulation is about your mental health. Can you take care of yourself? And if that means professional interventions, do that. What is going to work for you? I believe that we all have it in us to be mentally strong, but we have to be taught how, and then we have to practice it over and over.

Journal

Use this page to journal any thoughts and feelings you may be experiencing along your journey:

_____

_____

_____

_____

_____

_____

_____

_____

_____

_____

_____

_____

_____

_____

_____

_____

_____

_____

_____

_____

_____

_____

Now that you've completed your 45- day grief journey, keep going. Choose the time and frequency with which you will continue to actively grieve. I know that you, like me, have learned a lot about yourself and your truth. Carry on by attending to your 5 Self's. What happened to you was not okay, but you will be okay! See the appendix and our website for more information about the Mentally STRONG Method. Although you have suffered, you are becoming mentally stronger every day.

Dr. B's Controlled Grief and 5 SELF's Process Day 45

Controlled Grief: On the 1-year anniversary of Miah's death, I felt numb. I watched TV and someone was doing CPR which would usually cause a severe emotional reaction. I felt nothing.

- **Spiritual Self:** I meditated on being confident in finding and speaking my truth.
- **Self-Improvement:** I am committed to lifelong learning and growing.
- **Self-Movement:** There was minimal movement for me today because of pain.
- **Self-Regulation/Choose**: It is finished.
- **Self-Care:** I had to rest post-op. I let myself rest.

My Controlled Grief Journey Day 45

Date: / /

What is your mood today?
(circle or fill in your own word)

Open	Loving	Sad	Guilty
Calm	Present	Depressed	Afraid
Relaxed	Safe	Broken Hearted	Overwhelmed
Hopeful	Angry	Irritable	Exhausted
Connected	Furious	Longing	Drained
Strong	Resentful	Disconnected	Numb

What activity did you choose to practice for **Controlled Grief**? _____

_____

What have you done today to empower your **Spiritual Self**? _____

_____

How did you practice **Self-Regulation** today? _____

_____

How were you able to work on **Self-Improvement** today? _____

_____

How were you able to prioritize your **Self-Care**? _____

_____

How were you able to work on **Self-Movement** today? _____

_____

Any other thoughts you want to remember about your **journey** today?

_____

Choice Opportunity of the day:

Self-regulation is the Choice Opportunity for Day 45. I know that life feels like a rollercoaster, especially when you are experiencing intense grief and pain. Some days, you feel emotionally okay and then on other days, you feel absolutely horrible. This final Choice Opportunity is about how you can manage that rollercoaster. You must continue to do so as you move beyond these 45 days, and you will. You are Mentally STRONG.

Choice Opportunity: Self-Regulate

Do your emotions and mood feel like you are riding a scary roller coaster?

We cannot control much of what happens around us; yet, through utilizing the skill of self-regulation we can provide an internal balance to the external stressors of life.

How do you respond externally?	How do you respond internally?

The goal is to regulate your mood into a more normal pattern of ups and downs.

The emotional rollercoaster can be triggered by a traumatic incident or an overwhelming life event. Our external reactions often consume a significant amount of emotional energy, which leads to internal emotional disruption. This results in stress, anxiety or depression. By regulating your external reactions you can reduce the internal turmoil.

Internal Emotion	External Reaction	Choose an opposite reaction. Will this change the emotion?
angry	fight, yell, hit	take a deep breath, be respectful, keep my mouth shut, listen first

This is your Choice Opportunity to be *Mentally STRONG*®

Learn more about *The Mentally STRONG Method*: **1-800-55-STRONG ~ www.mentallystrong.com**

*The Mentally STRONG Method with Choice Opportunities© Author: Cristi Bundukamara – not for reproduction/distribution

Recap & Post 45 Days

I embarked on this journey first for myself. It was almost a year since my second child had died and I didn't believe that I was even beginning to scratch the surface on processing her death. So, I went into these 45 days taking care of myself but also documenting it in the hopes that I would find patterns and insights that I could share with others.

The first several days of my grief journey were kind of what I expected. I was grieving and crying while looking at pictures of my kids and taking in the pain. Then, on Day 7, I was hit with significant anger. Days 1- 6 were about choosing to grieve for me, but there were several layers that occurred after that. The first layer for me was anger. Everyone has an external layer to protect themselves. I went from Day 7 to around Day 22 working through the layers and insights that I gained. I found out that anger, or that protective outer layer, is just protecting us from the pain that is deeper. On Days 8, 9 and 10, I came to the realization that there's been a lot of traumas  surrounding my losses. My son Reggie was sick for many years with multiple hospitalizations and then ultimately died. I also found Miah dead and did CPR on her. I was in a trauma response for a long time. Trauma was another layer of grief for me. I'm not saying that everyone has the same layers, but I am saying that grief, in general, has layers. At that time, I realized that it was super important to incorporate the identify and organize portion of the Mentally STRONG method as I was working through those layers.

I also came to a point where there were some spiritual breakthroughs as well. I learned that I was beginning to heal but then hit bottom at around Day 17. I remembered once again that suicidal thoughts are a real thing in grief. I reminded myself that I could handle anything, though, and that suicide was not an option. Still, it was another layer and under that layer was the question of *Who am I without my children*? I had to dig deeper and realized that I needed to figure out who I am now and how to take care of myself (one more layer). I discovered that it is critical for me to learn how to be present as well (yet another layer). Depression was the final layer for me. Anger was on the outside, but depression related to the losses was deep inside of my body and soul.

As I went through processing my layers, I began to ask myself, *what is truth?* Around Day 23 and forward, I focused on it. I call this area of grief *finding my truth.* I went back to where I raised my kids and spent time with my family in hopes of trying to figure out what my truth is. There was a definite process to it, and I believe that I was able to start finding my truth, although it's a lifetime process.

Then towards the end of my 45 Days, I felt like I was starting from scratch. I was depressed and didn't want to do it anymore. I didn't want to go on without my children. It took me two or three days to lift myself out of that, but I was able to! I believe that grief relapses can happen (even multiple times) but knowing that you can turn it around and making the choice to pull yourself out is what matters. After that, I started thinking about how I was going to communicate all that I've discovered along my journey. I wanted to be able to relay the information in a way that best helped others, that's when I came up with the 5 Self's.

I want you to take this on as the next step in your grieving process because grief is not ever over. It is forever, but we can learn to grow around grief, and in spite of grief. We can manage and process the pain of it by making a personal vision related to Controlled Grief and the 5 Self's. I'm going to share with you my personal vision around each of those things. Then, I want you to make a personal vision for them as well. Creating a personal vision is your choice in terms of what you decide to do moving forward.

My Personal Vision Around Controlled Grief

My personal vision for Controlled Grief is that I can honor and respect my eternal connection to my children, and the purpose they had in my life and in this world. I will do that by taking action to actively grieve. That means feeling the pain but also choosing to find joy.

My Personal Vision for the 5 Self's

Self-care: My vision is to take care of myself physically, emotionally, and spiritually.
Self-regulation: My vision is to continue to learn to feel and manage my feelings and share techniques in order to learn to self-regulate. Some actions around that involve creating this book, putting together a grief documentary, and beginning to create a trauma book.
Spiritual Self: What can I do right now as I continue to take actions around healing myself spiritually? Throughout the whole 45 days, spiritual conflict came up a lot for me because I'm not okay with a loving protective God who has taken my children, but I am committed in my personal vision to continue to try to grow in the space.

Self-improvement: It is important that I first acknowledge that right now I am enough while still continuing to improve. I can do that by reading books and learning new things about my health or mental wellness and strength.

Self-movement: My plan here is two-fold. Movement promotes physical health, but it is also the way in which we process our grief and trauma. I am committed to continuing to move grief and trauma from my body. I can do that right now by finding activities that bring me joy as well as those that bring me peace.

I have mentioned several times throughout the 45 days that I encourage you to learn the Mentally STRONG Method, specifically around the identifying and organizing process. It's vital that we learn to compartmentalize when appropriate (doing so in an organized fashion that allows for growth in all areas). It is not compartmentalizing where you're putting it away, you are merely organizing it to better understand and address it.

I would like to share my own thoughts and feelings within each of these categories so that you have examples. **My core connection** is that I have often felt that I wasn't good enough. I wasn't good enough to save my children and the trauma associated with that is that, in my mind, hard work doesn't equal success. I did everything that I could to try to help them so the core connection there is that I'm not good enough. What is the power of choice there for me? It is to remind myself that I am good enough and that there was so much joy in purpose to their lives. I was a really good mother and caretaker.

My triggers. I often feel empathy. It doesn't trigger a negative emotional spiral for me, but I can sometimes get sad. Some things that cause a trigger for me are mothers that don't appreciate the amazing relationships that they have with their children or when I see a miracle where someone recovers from a really difficult disease or diagnosis. Although I am happy for other people, the trigger for me is *why didn't I get a miracle*? What I can do about it is to remind myself that I am enough. I am a good mother and there's an eternal connection with my children. I can also remind myself of all the work that I've done in these 45 days and will continue to do.

A **trigger** for my trauma is anyone that is in a life-threatening situation. I used to be a nurse in the ER, but I could never do that again. I hope that I don't ever come across someone that I need to perform CPR on. I recently had to renew my CPR certification and it actually caused me to have flashbacks to the day Miah died. I was not able to complete the certification as a result. So, what can I do about that? I can continue to work on those triggers. I can continue to define peace and avoid things like working in the ER.

By this point, I hope you are able to see the importance of **grief** being in its own category. In grief, we need to feel the pain, process the pain, and acknowledge that it will never go away. We must also get to a spot where we are able to cherish the good times. Now, if you're enmeshed in everything (your injustice, your spiritual conflict, your triggers, and your negative thoughts), there's no way you can cherish the positive things. But the relationship(s) that we've lost should be cherished. I would never go back in time and not have Reggie, Miah, and Johnny. Although it is so painful to have lost them, I cherished the time that I had with them. I cherish that they lived this life. I cherish the people that they have impacted. I cherish the life lessons that they chose and provided for me.

In the next category, **trauma**, I separated out 15 years of trauma from running Reggie to the hospital so many times including the day when he broke his femur in the middle of a seizure. Multiple times, doctors told me to give up, but I fought anyhow. I was ready to fight for Miah too, but Miah didn't give me a chance to fight. She never got that sick, but it was still very traumatic for me to do CPR on her (what I now know was) dead body.

We too must process trauma, but we don't want to cherish trauma, so separating my grief from my trauma was super important. As I process the trauma, I am separating myself from it. I'm trying to let it go. So, identifying what part of your grief was traumatic goes in this category because we're going to process that pain and attempt to remove ourselves from it. It's different from the pain of grief where we're going to cherish the relationship(s) and even the pain.

I'm moving into the next category of **negative thoughts**. We all have negative thoughts. Maybe they're negative thoughts towards yourself, or maybe they're negative thoughts towards others, or just general negativity. As you know, grief feeds those negative thoughts. There are times that I think I was a bad mother, or that I'm not smart enough, or that I didn't do enough. Sometimes I even start thinking, what's the point? After all, I've lost the most important things to me in the world. Those are all negative thoughts, and you can see how they can get enmeshed in grief. But negative thoughts are a choice, and they are something that I/we can control. So, the power of choice here for me is to take those thoughts captive and to not let them control me. I have to not let them impact my mood, behaviors, and choices.

What am I doing with my actions? Am I feeding into the pain of my grief and my negative thoughts, or am I trying to treat my depression and PTSD symptoms? That's a choice. There are so many things that are a choice. We had no control over losing our loved ones, but we have control and a choice about what we do moving forward. Every day I experience anxiety and worry. I'm constantly feeling like, what's next? Is my husband going to die? Is he going to pass quietly in his sleep or is it going to be some traumatic thing? Will he get sick? Will he need full care? These are the things that I worry about constantly.

It's not about getting rid of the anxiety; it's about decreasing its impact on your daily life. So, I try to live in the present. I am safe right now. My husband is safe. I try not to fuel the fire of anxiety by putting more anxiety on top of the already existing anxiety. It's like adding gas to a fire and not what we want to do.

The next category is **injustice**. It is not fair that I have had to fight DRPLA for 15 years. It is not fair that I have lost children and will likely lose my husband. Injustice has not been a huge category for me. It's been more of a spiritual conflict, but I have a friend who lost their child by the actions of a drunk driver, and they struggle with this category significantly. But what can you do about that? Don't let it get enmeshed with your negative thoughts, your trauma, and your grief. Injustice is about making a choice, dealing with your anger, and choosing what you're going to do about it. This friend spent a lot of time and energy to make sure that the drunk driver served time in jail. They also do things like participating in Mothers Against Drunk Driving and volunteer work around that. Those activities involve hope in this category of injustice. See how it's important to keep it separate and not to allow it to enmesh because the anger towards that drunk driver is not their grief. That is an injustice next to spiritual conflict which was one of the most significant things for me too. I have always felt like I had a relationship with God. I felt like I was a good person and good people should have good things happen to them. I started to feel like God had something against me and that I couldn't trust God. You've seen me work through that in my 45 days, and I will continue to work through that. I have found an eternal connection with my children. I have wrestled with God, but it is my choice that I will continue on that journey.

Last is the category of **addiction**. Sometimes in grief, we get addicted to the pain and we wallow in it. We have a right to be in pain and so often it's all we're going to feel. I challenge you there though.

We must also consider that there are other addictions to substances too. Be careful with alcohol and substances that numb the pain including the prescription medication that your doctor might give you. Some of those medications can mask that pain and cause addiction. Addiction to food is another thing. I jokingly say that I eat my pain but there's some truth to that. I have to be careful of not just trying to cover up my pain with an addiction. So, this is its own category because we want to acknowledge it. It's more than a behavior, there is a biochemical change that happens in addiction, the dopamine rewards system, so make choices not to feed into it. I don't go down the road of potential addiction with alcohol and you should watch out for these potential addictions too.

I applaud you for completing your 45 Day Controlled Grief Journey. You've processed the layers around your grief, identified what you must do for your own continued healing, and probably have a better understanding of who you are now (after the loss). Because you want to keep moving forward, remember and continue to work on your plan to do so (refer to your Personal Vision here as well). Part of this forward momentum and growth involves cherishing the relationship that you had with your loved one while continuing to honor your everlasting spiritual connection with them. That forward movement is also grounded in finding your truth. You will likely have relapses from time to time and that's okay; you now have a plan for how to deal with and get out of them. When experiencing anger, look for ways to release it and lean into the opposite anchor of gratitude. There is still much joy to be had in your life.

Forty-five days is not and will never be enough to completely get over your loss. Focus on taking care of your 5 Self's and scheduling Controlled Grief on days that are significant to you. With my final words, I strongly encourage you to learn the Mentally STRONG Method or maybe even get some professional help if needed to continue on your grief journey. Be sure to check out the additional resources from our Mentally STRONG Academy that will help you grow mentally stronger. I believe in you and your purpose. It will never be okay, but you will be okay. Trust yourself.

Appendix

The Mentally Strong Method (an Introduction)

Throughout this workbook, I referred to and included information and worksheets related to the Mentally STRONG Method which can be applied to grief. I created the Mentally STRONG Method because I truly believe we can strengthen our brains. Mental strength is an attribute we admire in people; however, we do not teach it in any standard curriculum. This method is scientifically backed by cognitive behavioral theories and empowers you to gain insight, resilience, and mental strength on your lifetime journey of self-improvement. The Mentally STRONG Method is a simple and practical method which utilizes evidence-based research as its foundation in the form of cognitive-behavioral therapy. Cognitive-behavioral therapy (CBT) has been widely used as a primary treatment that emphasizes choice in association with principals of mental and behavioral change (Beck, 2011; Lefebvre, 1981), resulting in physical changes in your brain. Brain imaging studies using functional magnetic resonance imaging (fMRI) have actually demonstrated CBT's ability to rewire whole areas of the brain, blood flow and neuronal activation (Duval et al. 2015). These results are incredible and demonstrate that we all have the power to learn this method and change the way that we think.

I challenge you to embark on the process of learning the Mentally STRONG Method and taking responsibility for your own mental health as you embark on your grief journey. With the use of the Mentally STRONG Method, you will be supported to achieve a healthy mental state so that you can deal with your grief and process your thoughts. This method will allow you to deal with both significant concerns as well as lesser daily struggles. Becoming mentally strong is a life-long, learning journey and is very important for those dealing with loss. You will be constantly evolving and changing with it as you grow.

Using the process, you map your thoughts in relation to your past (your story), identify and organize those thoughts, and then embrace your power to choose. Afterwards, armed with insight, you will be empowered to move forward toward a meaningful Personal Vision for yourself. The Mentally STRONG Method provides an opportunity for you to develop while grieving, helping yourself and others.

The Mentally STRONG Method consists of four elements and can be further simplified into three main concepts, or words: THINK, ORGANIZE, and CHOOSE. Here is a brief description of each of the four elements:

Element 1: The Thought Map

A Thought Map is a visual activity which will enable you to identify a central thought or feeling that you are experiencing or struggling with. On a worksheet, you will list this central thought or feeling along with the contributing factors tied to it. The purpose of the Thought Map is to help you gain insight into how your past thoughts and experiences are impacting your current thought processes. This involves THINKING without rumination. It can become comfortable to focus on our current problems, but the reality is that many dysfunctional thought patterns started in early childhood and are still evident in the many similar thoughts and feelings we experience today.

Element 2: Identify and Organize

In this element, you will pinpoint the important factors contributing to the identified central thought in your Thought Map and organize them into ten categories. The purpose of the identify and organize element is to learn how to ORGANIZE your thoughts.

Element 3: Power of Choice

In this element, you will identify where change is possible or desired in each category. Then, you will have the opportunity to decide how you can go about making those changes. I encourage you to use your Choice Opportunity Worksheets to assist you in processing and planning those choices (these worksheets are placed throughout this workbook).

The purpose of the Power of Choice section is more than just to CHOOSE. Its purpose is to be able to make those choices in organized categories. Many proponents of positive psychology will often say that you should just choose to think positive. This is both true and false. It is true that positive thinking will help reverse and rewire your negative thoughts, but it's also false because it won't help with your grief and trauma. Therefore, it's important to work through the items in each category differently.

Element 4: Personal Vision:

In this element, you will develop several empowering Personal Visions for multiple areas of your life so that you can achieve sustainable, healthy mental strength. The purpose of creating your Personal Vision is to help drive your CHOICES now. You want to make sure your decisions today are in line with what you want in your life and the kind of person that you want to become.

You can become more familiar with the Mentally STRONG method in the Discovering the Mentally STRONG method workbook. But, since we are referring to the process throughout this workbook and using pieces from it, I felt it was important to give you the basis and background of it so that you can understand and apply it to your grieving process (as applicable).

You are

Mentally STRONG®

Printed in Great Britain
by Amazon

27618547R00143